Lesson Plans for the Busy Librarian

Lesson Plans for the Busy Librarian

A Standards Based Approach for the Elementary Library Media Center

Volume 2

Joyce Keeling

LIBRARIES
UNLIMITED
A Member of the Greenwood Publishing Group

Westport, Connecticut • London

Library of Congress Cataloging-in-Publication Data

Keeling, Joyce.
    Lesson plans for the busy librarian : a standards based approach for the elementary
library media center / by Joyce Keeling.
      p.   cm.
    Includes bibliographical references and index.
    ISBN 1-59158-263-6
      1. Library orientation for school children—United States. 2. Information literacy—Study
and teaching (Elementary)—United States. 3. Elementary school libraries—Activity
programs—United States. 4. Media programs (Education)—United States. I. Title.
Z711.2.K36   2006
027.62'5—dc21   2001054379

British Library Cataloguing in Publication Data is available.

Library of Congress Catalog Card Number: 2001054379
ISBN: 1-59158-263-6

First published in 2006

Libraries Unlimited, 88 Post Road West, Westport, CT 06881
A Member of the Greenwood Publishing Group, Inc.
www.lu.com

Printed in the United States of America

The paper used in this book complies with the
Permanent Paper Standard issued by the National
Information Standards Organization (Z39.48–1984).

10 9 8 7 6 5 4 3 2 1

Dedication

This book is dedicated to all school librarian/teachers. A very special thanks goes to Verg, Chad, Jan, Adam, Rob, and Carisa Keeling, with an extra thanks to Jan for pushing the book ideas. Also thanks goes to Hinderene Van Raden, Rod and Teresa Van Raden, and finally to Deb and Sam Anderson.

Contents

Introduction

What a pleasure to have the privilege of writing a second volume of lesson plans for you, the busy library teacher! As you well know, it is so important for the library and teaching profession to have library lessons that are based on standards and benchmarks. As with the first volume, this second volume has lessons for kindergarten through fifth grade students that are first of all founded on solid standards and benchmarks, then built up around active and fun learning while focusing on individual student learning needs. These lessons are quick and easy to use for the busy librarian and other members of the teaching team. All lessons are designed to occupy approximately twenty minutes of instruction and have been successfully field tested with elementary library students. The easily prepared lessons are peppered with fun library learning skills needed to ensure successful, information-literate students. The importance of information literacy, and many statewide library studies, such as the surveys found at http://www.ala.org.aasl/SLMR/slmr_resources/select_lance.html or http://www.aea9.k12.ia.us/04/statewidelibrarystudy.php have proven how important library skills are.

Some define information literacy as the development of library skills and literary appreciation. This encompasses learning to successfully locate, assess, and use nonfiction and fiction sources in print and nonprint formats, learning to use databases, Internet, and the automated card catalog, and simply learning to enjoy and comprehend many genres of literature. Successful use of library sources creates successful lifelong learners of children as they develop problem-solving skills and decision-making ability. Every student should have the chance to succeed with his or her unique learning style. Howard Gardner defines the following learning styles, which are referenced in each lesson, in his theory of Multiple Intelligences of Learning. Gardner posits these intelligences, among others:

1. The mathematical learner who enjoys the challenge of math problems, computers, thinking logically, experimenting, and playing strategic games.

2. The linguistic learner who likes to write, tell stories, read, spell, do puzzles, and has a good memory for names, places, dates, and trivia.

3. The spatial leaner who likes to imagine, daydream, create with art and to draw, and enjoys movies or visuals. This learner also reads maps and thinks visually.

4. The musical leaner who translates language into rhythm, and enjoys music when studying.

5. The bodily kinesthetic learner who does well in sports, acting, and physical activities, needs to be active to learn, and uses the body for learning.

6. The interpersonal learner who learns better within groups and is good at contributing to group goals.

7. The intrapersonal learner who prefers to reflect as he or she learns, and acts individually.

Gardner has also added an eighth style, the naturalist learner who learns through different aspects of the environment.

Individual learning styles are one extremely important aspect of instruction, alongside the foundation provided by nationally recognized educational and professional standards. One such set of standards is the Information Literacy Standards of the American Association of School Librarians and the Association for Educational Communications and Technology (AASL/AECT):

1. Students are information literate when they access information efficiently and effectively.

2. Students are information literate when they evaluate information critically and competently.

3. Students are information literate when they use information effectively and creatively.

4. Students are independent learners and are information literate when they pursue information related to personal interests.

5. Students are independent learners and are information literate when they appreciate and enjoy literature and other creative expressions of information.

6. Students are independent learners and are information literate when they strive for excellence in information seeking and knowledge generation.

7. Students who contribute to the learning community and to society are information literate when they recognize the importance of information to a democratic society.

8. Students who contribute to the learning community and to society are information literate when they practice ethical behavior in regard to information and information technology.

9. Students who contribute to the learning community and to society are information literate when they participate effectively in groups to pursue and generate information.

Another set of national standards incorporated into each lesson is McREL, or the Kendall and Marzano National Standards and Benchmarks of the Mid-Continent Research for Education and Learning. The language arts standards of McREL are found in every lesson. Although school librarians and teachers must take care to follow the national standards, specific state and district standards should also be considered in using the lessons.

The lessons, grounded in standards, team teaching, and awareness of diverse learning styles, ensure that students' needs to become independent, information-literate learners are met in the classroom. Students will learn to appreciate literature and other sources of information and this will ensure them success in our world of global information and lifelong learning.

Joyce Van Raden Keeling
PreK–8 School Library Media Specialist

Chapter 1

Kindergarten Lesson Plans

A solid, professionally based library lesson plan is built around developmental needs of students at their grade level, around the Kendall and Marzano or McREL: National Education Language Arts Standards and Benchmarks, the AASL (American Association of School Libraries), and the AECT (Association for Educational Communications and Technology) Information Literacy Standards, and around the various learning styles of students found in Gardner's Multiple Intelligences framework. (The selected AASL/AECT standards and Gardner's Multiple Intelligences are fully described in the introduction.) All of the following lessons are built around these standards, benchmarks, and skills in order to ensure that all students appreciate different forms of literature are competent users of information, and so become information literate.

Each lesson plan includes student objectives, team teaching suggestions, and suggested sources. Furthermore, each lesson is designed to last approximately twenty minutes. All lessons have been field-tested. The lessons provide individual or small-group worksheet work and are designed to make library learning enjoyable, to be easily accomplished in a librarian's or library teacher's busy schedule, and to be grounded in solid standards and benchmarks. Each lesson has a direct reference to the following McREL standards and benchmarks, as well as a reference to the AASL/AECT standards.

Kindergarten Library Standards and Language Arts Benchmarks (McREL)

Reprinted by permission of McREL

Kindergarten students will be able to:

Use the general skills and strategies of the writing process. (Standard 1)

1. Use writing and other methods (e.g., using letters) to describe. (Standard 1, Benchmark 6)

Gather and use information for research purposes. (Standard 4)

2. Use a variety of sources to gather information (e.g., informational books, pictures, charts, indexes, videos, Internet). (Standard 4, Benchmark 2)

Use the general skills and strategies of the reading process. (Standard 5)

3. Use meaning clues (e.g., pictures) to aid in comprehension. (Standard 5, Benchmark 2)
4. Know the proper way to handle books. (Standard 5, Benchmark 4)
5. Know that books have titles, authors, and often illustrators. (Standards 5, Benchmark 12)

Use reading skills and strategies to understand and interpret a variety of literary texts. (Standard 6)

6. Use reading skills and strategies to understand a variety of familiar literary text (e.g., fairy tales, folktales, fiction, nonfiction, legends, fables, myths, poems, nursery rhymes, picture books, predictable books). (Standard 6, Benchmark 1)
7. Know the elements that compose a story (e.g. character, plot, events, setting). (Standard 6, Benchmark 2)
8. Know the difference between fact and fiction, real and make-believe. (Standard 6, Benchmark 4)

Use reading skills and strategies to understand and interpret a variety of informational texts. (Standard 7)

9. Use prior knowledge and experience to understand and respond to new information. (Standard 7, Benchmark 6, under grades 3–5)

Use listening and speaking strategies for different purposes. (Standard 8)

10. Create or act out familiar stories, rhymes, and plays. (Standard 8, Benchmark 9)

Take Care of Books!

Pick a picture. Color it, cut it out, and glue it at the top of the bookmark. On the rest of the bookmark, draw a picture about how to take care of books.

Take Care of Books!

Take Care of Books!

Standards

Students will

- Know the proper way to handle books. (McREL 4)
- Use reading skills and strategies to understand a variety of familiar literary text (e.g., fairy tales, folktales, fiction, nonfiction, legends, fables, myths, poems, nursery rhymes, picture books, predictable books). (McREL 6)
- Use prior knowledge and experience to understand and respond to new information. (McREL 9)
- Use information effectively and creatively. (AASL/AECT 3)
- Practice ethical behavior in regard to information. (AASL/AECT 8)

Objectives

After listening and looking at one or more nonfiction books, students discuss good library manners. Students create and color a bookmark.

Directions

1. The library teacher reads one or more books on manners and makes the connection to good library manners.
2. The library and language arts teachers explain how books should be handled. They demonstrate such things as turning pages carefully, having clean hands, keeping books dry, putting books in a safe place, and using a bookmark.
3. Students share book-care ideas based on their own experiences.
4. Students select and color a book-care picture from their sheets, and glue it near the top of the bookmark. On the rest of the bookmark, students illustrate book care.
5. The library teacher shows students how bookmarks are used and encourages them to display good manners in their next class!

Learning Styles

Spatial (coloring), intrapersonal (working alone), and linguistic (looking at the books and discussing).

Teaching Team

Social studies and library teachers.

Suggested Resources

Berenstain, Stan and Jan Berenstain. *The Berenstain Bears Forget Their Manners*. New York: Random House, 1985.

DeGezelle, Terri. *Manners at the Library*. Mankato, MN: Capstone, 2005.

Numeroff, Laura. *If You Take a Mouse to School*. New York: Laura Geringer, 2002.

Scary, Richard. *Pig Will, Pig Won't: A Book in Manners*. New York: Random House, 1985.

Going on a Train Ride

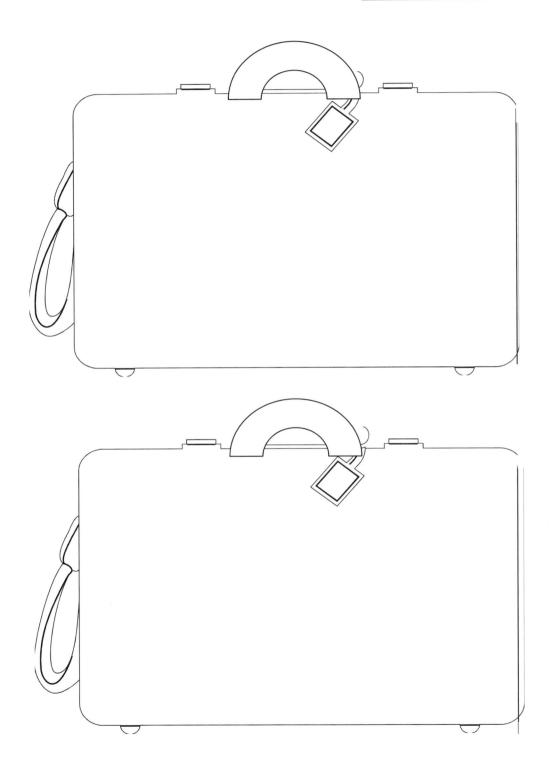

Going on a Train Ride

Standards

Students will

- Use meaning clues (e.g., pictures) clues as an aid in comprehension. (McREL 3)
- Use reading skills and strategies to understand a variety of familiar literary passages and text (e.g. fairy tales, folktales, fiction, nonfiction, legends, fables, myths, poems, nursery rhymes, picture books, predictable books). (McREL 6)
- Use information accurately and creatively. (AASL/AECT 3)
- Participate effectively in groups to pursue and generate information. (AASL/AECT 9)

Objectives

After listening to and looking at a nonfiction book, students discover facts about trains. Then students listen to and look at a fictional train story. Students draw imaginary things to take in their suitcases on a train ride.

Directions

1. The art and/or library teachers make copies of the student suitcase sheets on heavy-duty paper or cardstock.
2. The library teacher or social studies teacher reads and shows the illustrations of a nonfiction book on trains, and discusses train facts.
3. The teacher reads and shows the illustrations of a fiction train book, and discusses taking a train trip and what things to pack.
4. Students cut out their suitcases, then draws and colors on them, things to pack for an imaginary train trip. The art teacher may direct this activity.
5. The suitcases are stapled or taped together on the bottom only. The sides and top of the suitcases are unattached so they may be opened as needed on the "train trip."

Learning Styles

Spatial (imagining, coloring, drawing), intrapersonal (creating one's own suitcase items), interpersonal (gathering ideas from others), bodily kinesthetic (acting), mathematical (thinking logically), and linguistic (looking at and hearing books).

Teaching Team

Art, social studies, and library teachers.

Suggested Resources

Crebbin, June. *The Train Ride*. Cambridge, MA: Candlewick, 1999. [Fiction]
Meisel, Paul. *Engine, Engine Number Nine*. New York: Scholastic, 1998. [Fiction]
Simmon, Seymour. *Seymour Simmon's Book of Trains*. New York: HarperCollins, 2002. [Nonfiction]
Stille, Darlene R. *Freight Trains*. Minneapolis, MN: Compass Books, 2003. [Nonfiction]

Stop and Read!

 Stop signs tell us to stop, look, and listen! What would a sign in the library say?

Stop and Read!

Standards

Students will

- Use a variety of sources to gather information (e.g., information books, pictures, charts, indexes, videos, charts, indexes, videos, Internet) (McREL 2)
- Use meaning clues (e.g., pictures) to aid in comprehension. (McREL 3)
- Use prior knowledge and experience to understand and respond to new information. (McREL 9)
- Use information critically and competently. (AASL/AECT 3)

Objectives

Students discuss safety rules to follow while coming to school, while in the school, and while in the library. Students color and cut out stop signs.

Directions

1. The social studies teacher introduces this lesson on safety, discussing ways to be safe while coming to school on a bike or by walking, while in school, and of course while safely working in a library. Such discussions involve issues such as no running in the hallways, taking turns, and reminders to stop at stop signs when walking to school.

2. The library teacher reads and discusses a safety book. As the teacher is reading, students view the illustrations so that they can describe safety concepts from the picture clues.

3. The teacher asks students why there would be a stop sign in a library. Answers may include prohibiting running or simply to encourage stopping and reading.

4. Students color and cut out their stop signs. If they wish to attach them to a signpost, the art teacher may help by creating the signposts out of tightly wound newspapers or large sheets of construction paper rolled into long tubes.

5. After creating the signs, students recite a rhyme about stopping to read while holding their signs and marching. "Stop and read! It's the way to be! Do not run. Do not shout. Read, read, and read!"

Learning Styles

Spatial (coloring), interpersonal (working alone), and linguistic (finding picture clues).

Teaching Team

Art, social studies, and library teachers.

Suggested Resources

Hoban, Tana. *I Read Signs*. New York: Greenwillow, 1983.
Raatma, Lucia. *Safety on Your Bicycle*. Mankato, MN: Bridgestone, 1999.
Thomas, Pat. *I Can be Safe*. New York: Barrons, 2003.
Weber, Patricia. *Safety First*. Minneapolis, MN: Compass Books, 2004.

Tractors Go Farming

    Tractors help. Draw something behind the tractor so that it can help. Will you draw a plow? A wagon? What? Then color.

Tractors Go Farming

Standards

Students will

- Use a variety of sources to gather information (e.g., informational books, pictures, charts, indexes, videos, Internet). (McREL 2)
- Use meaning clues (e.g., pictures) to aid in comprehension (McREL 3)
- Evaluate information critically and competently. (AASL/AECT 2)
- Recognize the importance of information to a democratic society. (AASL/AECT 7)
- Participate effectively in groups to pursue and generate information. (AASL/AECT 9)

Objectives

Students discuss the uses of farm tractors. They draw something for the tractor to pull.

Directions

1. The social studies teacher will introduce this lesson by reading a fictional tractor book.
2. Using a nonfiction book or an encyclopedia, the library teacher shows ways that farm tractors are used (e.g., hauling wagons, pulling planters or plows).
3. Teachers show and discuss another nonfiction tractor source.
4. After brainstorming different ways that tractors can be used to help on the farm, students draw something hooked onto the tractor. For example, they could draw a wagon hooked to the tractor.
5. After completing their worksheets, students color their drawings. Students may end by singing "The Farmer in the Dale" as led by the music teacher.

Learning Styles

Linguistic (discussing facts), spatial (coloring), intrapersonal (drawing), interpersonal (sharing facts), and musical (singing).

Teaching Team

Music, library, and social studies teachers.

Suggested Resources

Conyer, David (director). *Vrrrooommm! Farming for Kids*. New York: Rainbow Communications, 1994. [Nonfiction video]

Cowley, Jo. *The Rusty, Trusty Tractor*. Minneapolis, MN: Sagebrush, 1999. [Fiction]

Harrington, Ray. *A Tractor Goes Farming*. St. Joseph, MO: America Society of Agricultural Engineers, 1995. [Nonfiction]

Kanno, Wendy. *The Farmer's Tractor*. Nearby, CT: Aro, 1993. [Fiction]

Strickland, Paul. *All About Tractors*. Milwaukee, WI: Gareth Stevens, 1990. [Nonfiction]

World Book Encyclopedia. Chicago, IL: World Book, 2004.

Turkeys

Turkeys

Standards

Students will

- Use a variety of sources to gather information (e.g., informational books, pictures, charts, indexes, videos, Internet). (McREL 2)
- Use meaning clues (e.g., pictures) as an aid in comprehension. (McREL 3)
- Know the difference between fact and fiction, real and make-believe. (McREL 8)
- Create or act out familiar stories, rhymes, and plays. (MCREL 10)
- Use information effectively and creatively. (AASL/AECT 2)
- Participate effectively in groups to pursue and generate information. (AASL/ECT 9)

Objectives

Students find facts about turkeys from a nonfiction book. Students color and create turkey hand puppets.

Directions

1. The science teacher introduces the lesson by reading a turkey fiction book.
2. The library teacher discusses and shows illustrations of two nonfiction sources about turkeys. The library teacher also emphasizes how the sources are nonfiction.
3. Students give 2- to 3-word turkey facts. These are written on the board. Each student chooses a fact and writes it on his or her hand band, located on the bottom of the worksheet.
4. Students color and cut out their turkeys and hand bands, and attach the turkeys to them.
5. Students put on their turkey hand puppets and act out being a turkey.

Learning Styles

Spatial (coloring), intrapersonal (coloring and acting alone), linguistic (discussing and viewing facts), interpersonal (sharing facts), and bodily kinesthetic (acting).

Teaching Team

Library and science teachers.

Suggested Resources

Arnosky, Jim. *All About Turkeys.* New York: Scholastic, 1998. [Nonfiction]

Balian, Lorna. *Sometimes It's Turkey—Sometimes It's Feathers.* Nashville, TN: Abingdon Press, 1986. [Fiction]

Brown, Marc. *Arthur's Thanksgiving.* Boston, MA: Little, Brown, & Co., 2000. [Fiction]

Cooper, Jason. *Turkey.* Vero Beach, FL: Rourke, 1995. [Fiction]

Saunders-Smith, Gail. *Turkeys on the Farm.* Mankato, MN: Capstone Press, 2002. [Nonfiction]

World Book Encyclopedia. Chicago, IL: World Book, 2004.

The Ants and the Grasshopper

> The Fable of the Ants and the Grasshopper:
> Grasshopper, "Please feed me!"
> The Ants, "No! You played when we worked."
> Moral: We must work when we can

1. Draw a line from the grasshopper to the fiddle that he will play.

2. What would you tell grasshopper?

3. Color the story.

The Ants and the Grasshopper

Standards

Students will

- Use writing and other methods (e.g., using letters) to describe. (McREL 1)
- Use reading skills and strategies to understand a variety of familiar literary passages and text (e.g., fairy tales, folktales, fiction, nonfiction, legends, fables, myths, poems, nursery rhymes, picture books, predictable books). (McREL 6)
- Use prior knowledge and experience to understand and respond to new information. (McREL 9)
- Appreciate and enjoy literature and other creative expressions. (AASL/AECT 5)
- Participate effectively in groups to pursue and generate information. (AASL/AECT 9)

Objectives

Students will hear and discuss a fable, while learning that a fable has a moral. Students will answer the worksheet questions.

Directions

1. The library teacher will explain that fables have something to teach us—a moral.
2. The library and reading teachers will read and lead discussions about "The Ant and the Grasshopper" fable. Discussions should lead in the direction of asking what could the ants have done differently (shared a bit)? Also students will answer what the grasshopper could have done differently.
3. Students will discuss worksheet questions. Simple class responses will be written on the board in one or two words. For example, when asked about the grasshopper, the class may want to write the word *work*. When done writing, they will color their sheets.
4. In the remaining time, students can hear another fable or view a fable video.

Learning Styles

Linguistic (writing), spatial (drawing, coloring), mathematical (thinking logically), interpersonal (discussing), and intrapersonal (working alone).

Teaching Team

Library and reading teachers.

Suggested Resources

Colman, Warren. *Aesop's Fables.* Niles, IL: United Learning, 1996. [Video]
Norio, Hikone. *Aesop's Fables—The Ant and the Grasshopper/Wind/Sun.* New York: Golden, 1991. [Video]
Winter, Milo. *The Aesop for Children.* New York: Barnes & Noble, 1993.
World Book Encyclopedia. *Childcraft Encyclopedia: The How and Why Library.* Chicago, IL: World Book, 2004.

Rhymes Make Me Laugh, Imagine That!

Rima, Jima Nickle.

Hearing rhymes makes me tickle.

Rima Jima Nickle.

We're in a pickle!

Elephant wants a hat.

Imagine that!

Rima Jima Tickle.

From Joyce Keeling, *Lesson Plans for the Busy Librarian: A Standards Based Approach for the Elementary Library Media Center*, Volume 2. Westport, CT: Libraries Unlimited. © 2006.

Rhymes Make Me Laugh, Imagine That!

Standards

Students will

- Create or act out familiar stories, rhymes, and plays. (McREL 10)
- Appreciate and enjoy literature and other creative expression. (AASL/AECT 7)

Objectives

Students recognize the rhythm of rhyming books. Students color an elephant, put a hat on it, and become familiar with the elephant rhyme.

Directions

1. The reading teacher and the library teacher read rhyming fiction books, stressing the rhythm in each book.
2. The library teacher reads the rhyme on the student worksheet.
3. Students color their worksheets, then choose a hat for the elephant, cut it out, and glue it on the elephant.
4. Students repeat the elephant rhyme until they are familiar with it.

Learning Styles

Linguistic (hearing stories), musical (rhythm), and spatial (coloring).

Teaching Team

Library and reading teachers.

Suggested Resources

Appelt, Kathi. *Bat Jamboree*. New York: William Morrow, 1996.
Martin, Bill. *Brown Bear, Brown Bear, What Do You See?* New York: Henry Holt and Company, 1992.
Martin, Bill Jr. *"Fire, Fire," Said Mrs. McGuire*. New York: Harcourt Brace, 1996.
Miranda, Anne. *The Elephant at the Waldorf*. Mahwah, NJ: Bridgewater, 1995.
Shaw, Nancy. *Sheep Take a Hike*. Boston, MA: Houghton Mifflin, 1994.
Seuss, Dr. [Theodor Geisel]. *Fox in Socks*. New York: Random House, 1993.
Seuss, Dr. [Theodor Geisel]. *Hop on Pop*. New York: Random House, 2001.
Thomas, Patricia. *"Stand Back," Said the Elephant, "I'm Going to Sneeze!"* New York: Lothrop, Lee & Shepard, 1990.

Making a Snowman

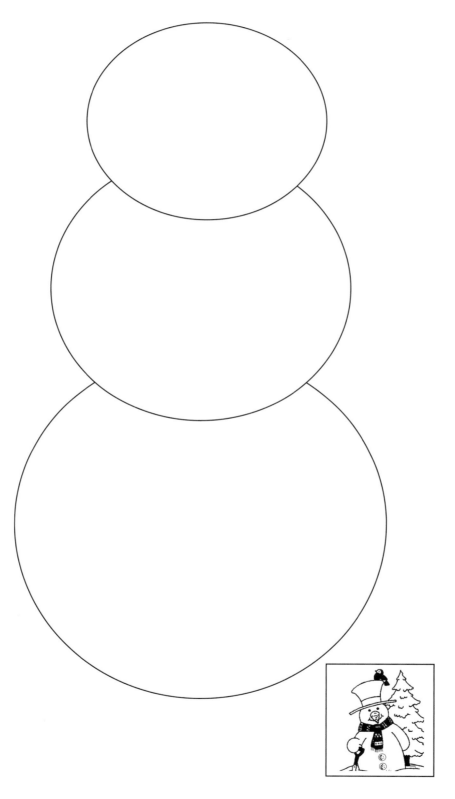

Making a Snowman

Standards

Students will

- Use meaning clues (e.g., pictures) to aid in comprehension. (McREL 3)
- Know the elements that compose a story (e.g. character, plot, events, setting). (McREL 7)
- Appreciate and enjoy literature and other creative expressions of information. (AASL/AECT 5)

Objectives

Students identify plot, setting, and main characters after hearing two snowman books. Students gather ideas on how to decorate a snowman while being shown the book illustrations. Students decorate and complete a snowman.

Directions

1. The library teacher reads two snowman books. As the teacher is reading, the illustrations are shown to the students to give them ideas for their activity.
2. Students discuss plot, setting, and main characters from each book.
3. The art or library teacher points out that the snowman on the worksheet doesn't have any facial features or other decorations. Students are directed to decorate and "make" their snowman.

Learning Styles

Linguistic (listening to stories), interpersonal (discussing), intrapersonal (creating alone), and spatial (decorating).

Teaching Team

Art and library teachers.

Suggested Resources

Briggs, Raymond. *The Snowman*. New York: Random House, 1989.
Buchner, Carolyn. *Snowman at Night*. New York: Dial Books, 2002.
Cuyler, Margery. *The Biggest, Best Snowman*. New York: Scholastic, 1998.
Goffstein, M.B. *Our Snowman*. New York: Harper & Row, 1986.
Sams, Carl II. *Stranger in the Woods*. Milford, MI: Jean Stoick, 2000.

GRRRR

GRRRR

Standards

Students will

- Use meaning clues (e.g., pictures) as an aid in comprehension. (McREL 3)
- Know the elements that compose a story (e.g., character, plot, events, setting). (McREL 7)
- Know the difference between fact and fiction, real and make-believe. (McREL 8)
- Create or act out familiar stories, rhymes, and plays. (McREL 10)
- Evaluate information critically and competently. (AASL/AECT 2)
- Participate effectively in groups to pursue and generate information. (AASL/AECT 9)

Objectives

Students are aware of the differences between fiction and nonfiction books after viewing, listening to, and discussing a fiction and nonfiction book on bears. Students create bear puppets and act out the story in the fiction book.

Directions

1. Students will need small paper sacks to make puppets.
2. The library teacher reviews that fiction is not real and nonfiction is real. The teacher reads a fictional bear story while showing the illustrations to demonstrate the fiction.
3. The science teacher then reads a nonfiction bear book while showing the pictures and pointing out bear facts.
4. Students summarize the differences between fiction and nonfiction.
5. Students make a bear sack puppet by coloring the bear on the worksheet and attaching it to a small paper sack.
6. Using their puppets, the students act out the bear character from the fiction book.

Learning Styles

Spatial (coloring), interpersonal (working with others), linguistic (viewing and discussing books), mathematical (thinking logically), and bodily kinesthetic (acting).

Teaching Team

Library and science teachers.

Suggested Resources

Down, Mike. *Bear.* Mahwah, NJ: Troll, 1994. [Nonfiction]
Jorgensen, Gail. *Gotcha!* New York: Scholastic, 1995. [Fiction]
Kulling, Monica. *Bears in the Wild.* New York: Golden Books, 1998. [Nonfiction]
Rosen, Michael. *We're Going on a Bear Hunt.* New York: Margaret McElderry Books, 1989. [Fiction]
Stone, Lynn. *Brown Bears.* Minneapolis, MN: Lerner, 1998. [Nonfiction]

Christmas Stars

In the big dark night, (Point to sky)
Stars are shining bright. (Open hands wide)
Shining for me. (Point to self)
Shining for you. (Point to others)

On my Christmas tree, (Point to a corner)
There is a star made by me. (Point to self and then corner)
Shining for me. (Point to self)
Shining for you. (Point to others)

Stars are shining just everywhere! (Throw hands wide)

Christmas Stars

Standards

Students will

- Know the elements that compose a story (e.g., character, plot, events, setting). (McREL 7)
- Create or act out familiar stories, rhymes, and plays. (McREL 10)
- Appreciate and enjoy literature and other creative expression. (AASL/AECT 5)

Objectives

Students learn a rhyme about a star. They hear Christmas tree stories and identify the plot. Students decorate a star for Christmas.

Directions

1. Copy the student stars worksheet onto heavy or cardstock-type paper.
2. The reading and library teachers read two fiction books featuring Christmas trees.
3. The library teacher leads a discussion on the main plot of each story after the books are read.
4. Students repeat their action worksheet rhymes two or three times until they are familiar with it.
5. The art teacher helps students decorate their stars to be put on a tree.
6. After decorating their stars, students may repeat their rhymes once again.

Teaching Team

Art, library, and reading teachers.

Learning Styles

Linguistic (hearing stories), musical (rhyming), bodily kinesthetic (acting), spatial (coloring), interpersonal (discussing), and intrapersonal (decorating stars).

Teaching Team

Library and reading teachers.

Suggested Resources

Jasin, Janie. *The Littlest Christmas Tree*. Minneapolis, MN: Book Peddlers, 1996.
Pipper, Christie. *A Very Scraggly Tree*. Milwaukee, WI: Raintree, 1989.
Repchuk, Caroline. *The Snow Tree*. Singapore: Templar, 1996.
Quindlen, Anne. *The Tree That Came to Stay*. New York: Crown Publishers, 1992.

What Happened, Chicken Little?

What happened in the story? Draw a line from 1st, 2nd, and 3rd to the matching story box. Then color the story boxes.

What Happened, Chicken Little?

Standards

Students will

- Use meaning clues to gather information(e.g., pictures). (McREL 3)
- Use reading skills and strategies to understand a variety of familiar literary passages and text (e.g., fairy tales, folktales, fiction, nonfiction, legends, fables, myths, poems, nursery rhymes, picture books, predictable books). (McREL 6)
- Know the elements that compose a story (e.g., character, plot, events, setting). (McREL 7)
- Appreciate and enjoy literature and other creative expressions of information. (AASL/AECT 5)
- Strive for excellence in information seeking and knowledge generation. (AASL/AECT 6)

Objectives

Students explain plot, main characters, setting, and the order of events in the story of *Chicken Little*. Students identify the sequence of events of the story.

Directions

1. The library teacher reads and shows illustrations of *Chicken Little*. The library teacher pauses while reading to ask students what happens next.
2. Then the reading teacher has students explain the plot, setting, main characters, and the sequence of the story events.
3. On their worksheets, students draw a line from a number to the corresponding picture to explain the order of events in the story. Students color their worksheets.
4. Students check their worksheets to make sure they have everything accurate.
5. Teachers ask students how they might change the story.
6. If there is time, students may view the *Chicken Little* video recording.

Learning Styles

Linguistic (hearing a story, discussing), spatial (coloring), intrapersonal (working alone), interpersonal (discussing in groups), and mathematical (thinking logically).

Teaching Team

Library and reading teachers.

Suggested Resources

Hobson, Sally. *Chicken Little*. New York: Aladdin, 2000.
Kellogg, Steven. *Chicken Little*. New York: Morrow, 1987.
Kellogg, Steven. *Chicken Little*. Norwalk, CT: Weston Woods, 1998. [Video]
Sullivan, Maureen and Laura Rader. *Chicken Little*. New York: Harper, 1998.

Pigs

Pigs

Standards

Students will

- Know that books have titles, authors, and sometimes illustrators. (McREL 5)
- Know the elements that compose a story (e.g., character, plot, events, setting). (McREL 7)
- Create or act out familiar stories, rhymes, and plays. (McREL 10)
- Appreciate and enjoy literature and other forms of creative expression. (AASL/AECT 5)

Objectives

Students hear and discuss two fiction books featuring pigs, learning the title, author, and plot. Students create pig eye masks and act out the plot.

Directions

1. Copy student pig sheets onto card stock or heavy-duty paper. The eyes of the pig masks may be cut out ahead of time.
2. The library teacher defines the terms *author* and *title*. The reading teacher and the library teacher each read a fiction book featuring pigs, pointing out the title and author.
3. After reading the books, teachers check for understanding and ask students to define title and author. Students also explain the main characters in the plot.
4. Students color and cut out their pig eye masks.
5. Students hold their eye masks while acting, or they may make a headband to wear the mask on their faces (in Art class). Students may also make their own tails out of construction paper.
6. The library teacher reviews the main plot of each story and has students act it out with their pig masks. Small groups may watch as each student performs.

Learning Styles

Linguistic (discussing), spatial (creating, coloring), intrapersonal (acting), and bodily kinesthetic (acting).

Teaching Team

Art, library, and reading teachers.

Suggested Resources

Falconer, Ian. *Olivia*. New York: Atheneum Books, 2000.
Hobbie, Holly. *Toot and Puddle*. Boston, MA: Little, Brown and Company, 1997.
McPhail, David. *Pigs Aplenty, Pigs Galore!* New York: Dutton, 1993.
Plourde, Lynn. *Pigs in the Mud in the Middle of the Road*. New York: Blue Sky Press, 1997.
Teague, Mark. *Pigsty*. New York: Scholastic, 1994.

Marking the Page with Love

Make a Valentine Book Marker
Color the hearts. Glue on the words.

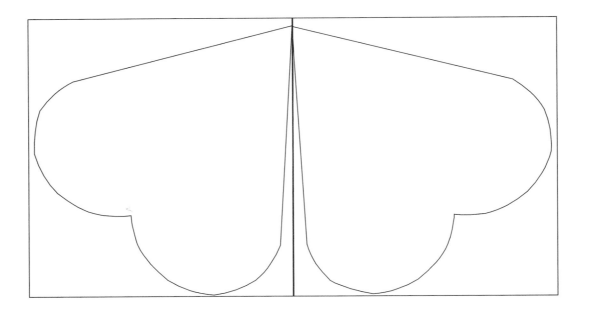

Marking the Page With Love

Standards

Students will

- Use meaning clues (e.g., pictures) to aid in comprehension. (McREL 3)
- Know that books have titles, authors, and often illustrators. (McREL 5)
- Use prior knowledge to understand and respond to new information. (McREL 9)
- Appreciate and enjoy literature and other creative expressions. (AASL/AECT 5)
- Participate effectively in groups to pursue and generate information. (AASL/AECT 9)

Objectives

Students review books. They show caring for others by creating Valentine page holders. They also review the concepts of title, author, and illustrator.

Directions

1. The library teacher reads a couple of books about caring and about Valentines Day, pointing out the author, title, and illustrator of each book.
2. Students discuss caring as shown in the books.
3. The art teacher leads the class in coloring the Valentine page markers. The "Be My Valentine Hearts" are colored, decorated, and glued to each page marker. The page markers are cut out.
4. Students fold the Valentine squares or page markers in half.
5. The library teacher shows students how the Valentine page markers fit on book pages, reminding them that this is a way to care for books.
6. Teachers tell students that they may give the markers to someone else.

Learning Styles

Linguistic (hearing stories and discussing), intrapersonal (working alone), and spatial (creating).

Teaching Team

Art and library teachers.

Suggested Resources

Bond, Felicia. *The Day It Rained Hearts*. New York: Laura Geringer Books, 2002. (Previously published as *Four Valentines in a Rainstorm*)

Capucilli, Alyssa Smith. *Biscuit's Valentine's Day*. New York: HarperCollins, 2001.

Cocca-Leffler, Maryann. *Lots of Hearts*. New York: Grosett & Dunlap, 1996.

Hudson, Eleanor. *The Best Thing About Valentines*. New York: Scholastic, 2004.

Hurd, Thacher. *Little Mouse's Big Valentine*. New York: Harper, 1990.

Fun with Mother Goose

Draw something fun on the little rhyme booklets. Put them in the basket.

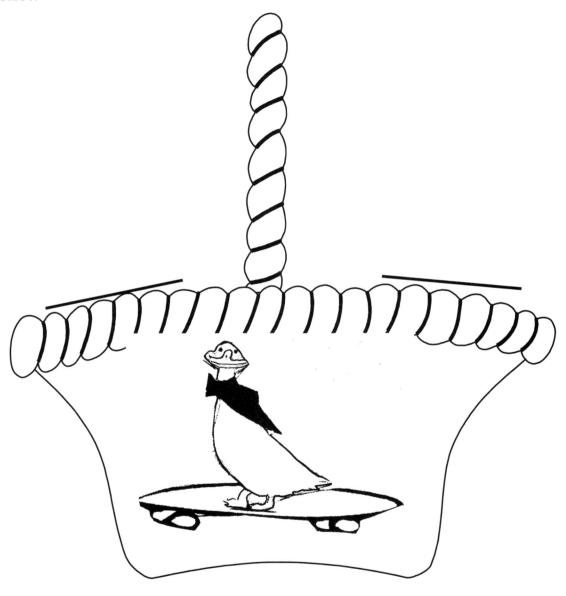

Jack be nimble, Jack be quick. Jack jump Over the Candlestick!		Little Boy Blue, Come blow your Horn, for the Sheep Are in the Meadow, And the cows, In the corn!	

Fun with Mother Goose

Standards

Students will

- Use writing and other methods (e.g., using letters) to describe. (McREL 1)
- Use reading skills and strategies to understand a variety of familiar literary passages and forms (e.g., fairy tales, folktales, fiction, nonfiction, legends, fables, myths, poems, nursery rhymes, picture books, predictable books). (McREL 6)
- Use information effectively and creatively. (AASL/AECT 3)
- Pursue information related to personal interests (choosing rhymes). (AASL/AECT 4)
- Appreciate and enjoy literature. (AASL/AECT 5)

Objectives

Students hear and recite some humorous and traditional rhymes. Students illustrate the rhymes to create two mini-rhyming booklets.

Directions:

1. Slit the black, bold slots before class.
2. The library and reading teachers read various humorous nursery rhymes and have the students repeat them.
3. Teachers read the two traditional rhymes on the student worksheet boxes.
4. Students illustrate the rhymes on the blank sides of the boxes with colorful and humorous drawings; the boxes then become rhyming booklets.
5. Students color the basket with Mother Goose riding her skateboard.
6. Students cut around the edges of the two rhyming booklets without separating the two boxes (pages). The booklets are folded in half.
7. Simple illustrations are added on the covers (the folded sides) of the booklets. The booklets fit into the slits in the Mother Goose basket.

Learning Styles

Linguistic (repeating rhymes), spatial (coloring, creating), intrapersonal (working alone), and musical (rhymes).

Teaching Team

Library and reading teachers.

Suggested Resources

Bell, Edward (director). *Mother Goose. A Rappin & Rhymin*. New York: HBO, 1997. [Video]
Lanksy, Bruce. *Mary Had a Little Jam and Other Silly Rhymes*. New York: Simon & Schuster, 2004.
Lansky, Bruce. *The New Adventures of Mother Goose: Gentle Rhymes for Happy Times*. New York: Simon & Schuster, 1993.
Opie, Iona. *My Very First Mother's Goose*. Cambridge, MA: Candlewick, 1996.
[Various artists] *Vol. 1—Mother Goose Rocks*. New York: Lightyear, 2000. [CD]

Sailing with the ABCs

The boat has ABCs on it. Find and color them.

Find an Easy book. Circle the ABC letter of the shelf:

A B C D E F G H I J K L M N O P Q R S T U V W X Y Z

Sailing with the ABCs

Standards

Students will

- Use writing and other methods (e.g., using letters) to describe. (McREL 1)
- Use prior knowledge and experience to understand and respond to new information. (McREL 9)
- Access information efficiently and effectively. (AASL/AECT 1)
- Strive for excellence in information seeking and knowledge. (AASL/AECT 6)

Objectives

Students hear ABC stories. They become aware of the location of Easy books in the library. They color the alphabet letters on the sailboat.

Directions

1. The library teacher points out that Easy books are in ABC order in the library, and shows students the alphabetical location of various Easy books.
2. The reading teacher reads one or two ABC books.
3. After hearing the ABC books, students find and color the ABCs on the sailboat worksheet.
4. Students then find an easy book and point out its ABC shelf location letter on their sheets by circling the letter.
5. If there is time, students may listen to another Easy alphabet book.

Learning Styles

Linguistic (hearing stories), mathematical (challenge of finding letters), spatial (coloring), bodily kinesthetic (finding a book and letter), and intrapersonal (working alone).

Teaching Team

Library and reading teachers.

Suggested Resources

Aylesworth, Jim. *Old Black Fly*. New York: Henry Holt,1995.
Floca, Brian. *The Racecar Alphabet*. New York: Atheneum, 2003.
Inkpen, Mick. *Kipper's A to Z*. New York: Red Wagon, 2000.
Johnson, Stephen. T. *Alphabet City*. New York: Viking, 1995.
Martin, Bill Jr. *Chicka, Chicka Boom Boom*. New York: Simon & Schuster, 1989.
Neumeier, Marty and Bryon Glaser. *Action Alphabet*. New York: Scholastic, 1985.

The Goose and the Golden Eggs

There is a fable about golden eggs. There was a farmer and his wife who had a goose that laid golden eggs. The farmer wanted more. The farmer thought he could get more golden eggs! But when he tried, it did not work for him.

He did not get any more golden eggs. He found out that he should have been happy with what he had.

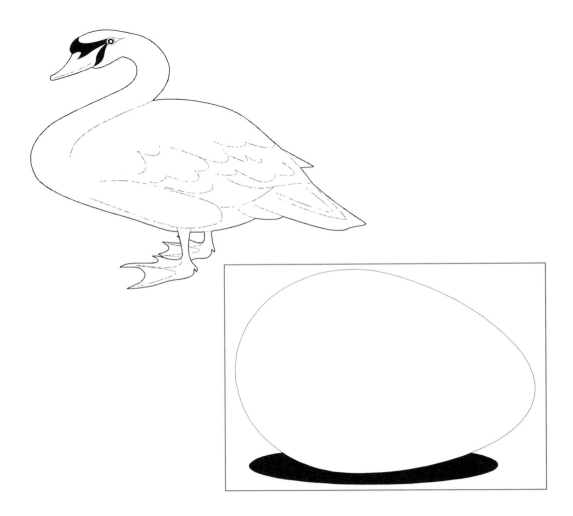

1. On the egg draw what happened to the farmer and his wife when their goose was laying golden eggs.

2. How did the couple feel when there were no more golden eggs? ☺ or ☹

3. What could the farmer have done instead?

The Goose and the Golden Eggs

Standards

Students will

- Use writing and other methods (e.g., using letters) to describe. (McREL 1)
- Use reading skills and strategies to understand a variety of familiar literary passages and text (e.g. fairy tales, folktales, fiction, nonfiction, legends, fables, myths, poems, nursery rhymes, picture books, predictable books). (McREL 6)
- Know the elements of a story (e.g., character, plot). McREL 7
- Use prior knowledge and experience to understand and respond to new information. (McREL 9)
- Recognize the importance of information to a democratic society. (AASL/AECT 7)
- Participant effectively in groups to pursue and generate information. (AASL/AECT 9)

Objectives

Students hear and then discuss the fable of "The Goose and the Golden Eggs" and its moral. They will draw the main plot on the egg. They will also hear a book on sharing.

Directions

1. The library teacher tells students to listen for the moral as they hear the fable of *The Goose That Laid the Golden Egg*.
2. After hearing the fable, students discuss main character, setting, plot, ending, and moral.
3. The teachers read and guide worksheet questions. On the worksheet egg, students draw and color a picture of what happened to the characters. Students discuss their feelings. After discussing the moral, students discuss what the farmer could have changed about his behavior (he could have shared), and then color the word *share*.
4. The reading teacher reads a book on the subject of sharing, such as *Selfish Sophie!, Franklin and the Scooter, Shelia Rae's Peppermint Stick,* or *Anna Shares.*

Learning Styles

Linguistic (writing), intrapersonal (working alone), mathematical (thinking logically), and spatial (drawing and coloring).

Teaching Team

Library and reading teachers.

Suggested Resources

Baker, Barbara. *Anna Shares.* New York: Dutton Children's Books, 2004.
Henkes, Kevin. *Shelia Rae's Peppermint Stick.* New York: HarperCollins, 2001.
Jennings, Sharon. *Franklin and the Scooter.* Toronto: Kids Can Press, 2004.
Kelleher, Damien. *Selfish Sophie!* Minneapolis, MN: Picture Window Books, 2003.
Pinkney, Jerry. *Aesop's Fables.* New York: Seastar Books, 2000.
White, Mark. *The Goose That Laid the Golden Egg.* Minneapolis, MN: Picture Window Books, 2004.

Counting the Dots

What is it? Connect the numbers. Make it into something by adding ears, eyes, and other things. Color it.

It is a _____.

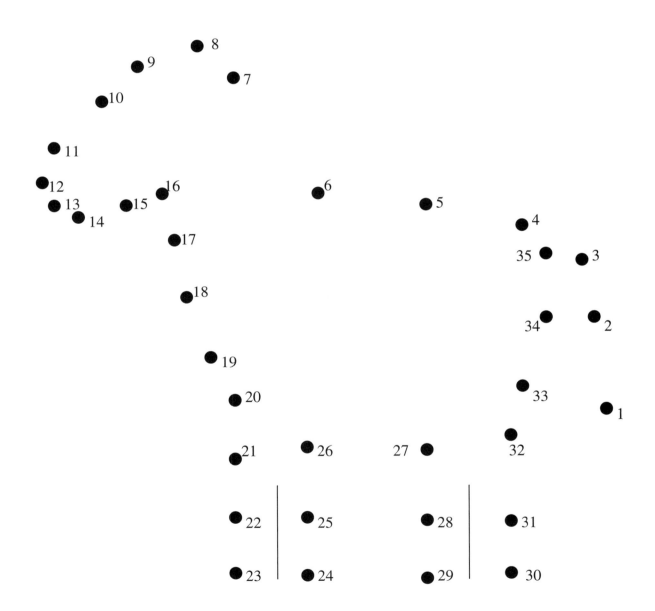

Counting the Dots

Standards

Students will

- Use a variety of sources to gather information (e.g., informational books, pictures, charts, indexes, videos, Internet). (McREL 2)
- Use meaning clues to aid in comprehension. (McREL 3)
- Use prior knowledge and experience to understand and respond to new information. (McREL 9)
- Appreciate and enjoy literature and other creative expressions of information. (AASL/AECT 5)

Objectives

Students listen to counting books as they are read to them. Students complete a connect-the-dots puzzle sheet by counting numbers on their own.

Directions

1. The library teacher reads two counting books to students.
2. The math teacher leads the dot-to-dot worksheet.
3. Students add facial features and other details to the connect-the horse figure.
4. Teachers write the word *horse* on the board so students may copy it.
5. If there is time, students may play an online math game with the assistance of their teachers.

Learning Styles

Spatial (puzzles, coloring), intrapersonal (working alone), mathematical (completing math), and linguistic (following along with the stories).

Teaching Team

Library and math teachers.

Suggested Resources

Bang, Molly. *Ten, Nine, Eight*. New York: William Morrow. 1983.

Christelow, Eileen. *Five Little Monkeys Jumping on the Bed*. Boston, MA: Houghton Mifflin, 1989.

Crews, Donald. *Ten Black Dots*. New York: William Morrow, 1986.

O'Keefe, Susan Heyboer. *One Hungry Monster: A Counting Book in Rhyme*. Boston, MA: Little, Brown and Company, 1989.

Tudor, Tasha. *1 is for One*. New York: Simon and Schuster, 1984.

Wise, William. *Ten Sly Piranhas*. New York: Dial, 1993

Online math games for Kindergarten students: http://www.primarygames.com/math/fishycount [online resource]

Duck Goes Swimming

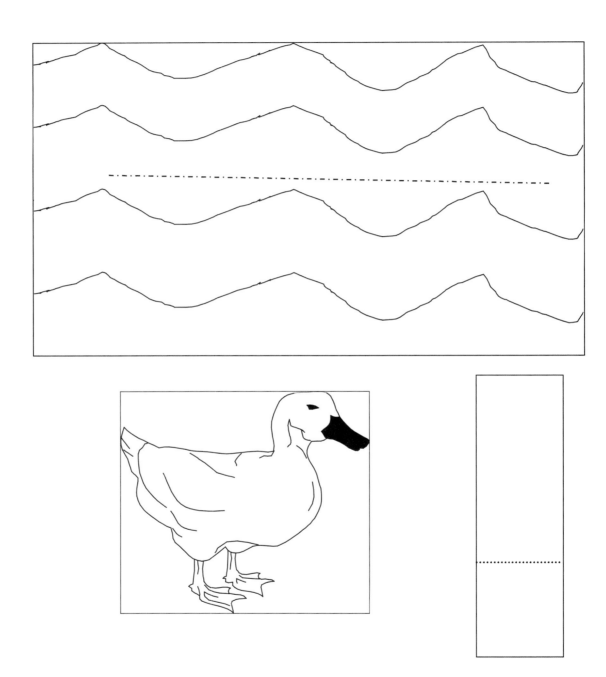

Duck Goes Swimming

Standards

Students will

- Use writing and other methods (e.g. using letters) to describe. (McREL 1)
- Use meaning clues (e.g. pictures) to aid in comprehension. (McREL 3)
- Know the difference between fact and fiction, real and make believe. (McREL 8)
- Evaluate information critically and competently. (AASL/AECT 2)
- Participate effectively in groups to pursue and generate information. (AASL/AECT 9)

Objectives

Students demonstrate knowledge of fiction and nonfiction differences. Students explain and write a simple duck fact. Students color and cut out the water square and duck, and attach it to the picture.

Directions

1. The library teacher reads a fiction duck book and discusses the term fiction.
2. The science teacher reads a nonfiction duck book and discusses nonfiction.
3. The differences between fiction and nonfiction are reviewed with the library teacher.
4. Teachers review duck facts from the nonfiction book, then students write a duck fact on their worksheets.
5. Students color and cut out the water, the duck square, and the strip. Teachers' help students bend the strip at the dotted line and attach the small part of the strip to the ducks' back, and then thread it through the cut dotted line so that the duck appears to swim.
6. If there is time, another duck fiction book or video may be used.

Learning Styles

Spatial (coloring), intrapersonal (working alone), linguistic (finding facts), and bodily kinesthetic (making duck swim).

Teaching Team

Library and science teachers.

Suggested Resources

Cronin, Doreen. *Giggle, Giggle, Quack.* New York: Simon Schuster, 2002. [Fiction]
Flack, Marjorie. *The Story About Ping.* [Video] Norwalk, CT: Weston Woods, 1995.
Gibbons, Gail. *Ducks.* New York: Holiday House, 2001. [Nonfiction]
Goldin, Augusta. *Ducks Don't Get Wet.* New York: HarperCollins, 1989. [Nonfiction]
Pizer, Abigall. *Percy the Duck.* Minneapolis, MN: Carolrhoda Books, 1997. [Fiction]
Stone, Lynn M. *Ducks.* Vero Beach, Fl: Rourke, 1990. [Nonfiction]
Waddell, Martin. *Webster J. Duck.* Cambridge, MA: Candlewick, 2004. [Fiction]

Carry a Zoo!

Color the animals. Choose an animal to put in your zoo! Put the animal in your zoo cage. Cut out the cage with the handle!

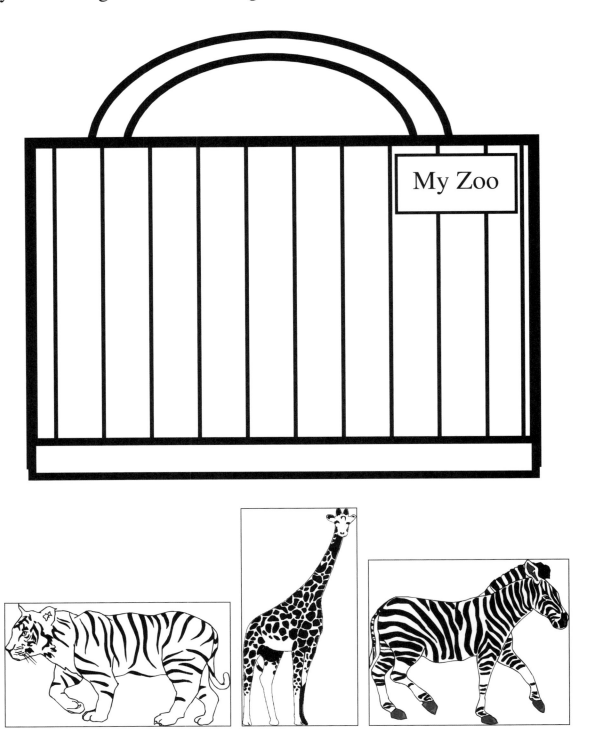

Carry a Zoo!

Standards

Students will

- Use meaning clues (e.g., pictures) to aid in comprehension. (McREL 3)
- Know that books have titles, authors, and often illustrators. (McREL 5)
- Use reading skills and strategies to understand a variety of familiar literary passages and text (e.g. fairy tales, folktales, fiction, nonfiction, legends, fables, myths, nursery rhymes, picture books, predictable books). (McREL 6)
- Use information effectively and creatively. (AASL/AECT 3)
- Recognize the importance of information to a democratic society. (AASL/AECT 7)
- Participate effectively in groups to pursue and generate information. (AASL/AECT 9)

Objectives

Students hear zoo books and discuss zoo animals. They review author and title. Students color and cut out an animal of their choice and their portable zoo.

Directions

1. The library or science teacher reads and discusses two books about the zoo. Illustrations are shown. Before reading each book, the author and title are pointed out and briefly discussed.
2. After hearing the stories, students discuss different animals seen in the zoo books.
3. Students color and cut out the zoo animals and the zoo cage from their worksheets and glue an animal in the zoo cage. Students carry their zoos.

Learning Styles

Linguistic (finding facts), intrapersonal (working alone), interpersonal (discussing), and spatial (coloring).

Teaching Team

Library and science teachers.

Suggested Sources

Aliki. *My Visit to the Zoo*. New York: HarperTrophy, 1999.
Carle, Eric. *1, 2, 3 to the Zoo*. New York: Philomel, 1996.
Fowler, Allan. *Animals in the Zoo*. Chicago, IL: Children's Press, 2000.
Gibbons, Gail. *Zoo*. New York: HarperTrophy, 1991.
Paxton, Tom. *Going to the Zoo*. New York: HarperTrophy, 1996.

Gone Fishing?

Gone Fishing?

Standards

Students will

- Know the elements that compose a story (e.g., character, plot, events, setting). (McREL 7)
- Use prior knowledge and experience to understand and respond to new information. (McREL 9)
- Use information effectively and creatively. (AASL/AECT 3)
- Pursue information related to personal interests. (AASL/AECT 4)
- Appreciate and enjoy literature and other creative expressions of information. (AASL/AECT 5)

Objectives

Students hear two summer books and discuss the main plot. Students brainstorm summer fun ideas. Students draw and color summer plans or thoughts on the fish.

Directions

1. Students hear two fiction books about summer vacation or summer fun as read by the reading and library teachers. Discuss main plot from each book.
2. Students explain the summer fun from the books. They brainstorm fun things done in the summer, such as vacations, swimming, fishing, bike riding, and reading.
3. On their worksheet fish, students draw and color pictures of the things that they like to do in the summer.
4. In art class, the fish may be cut out and hung by string or yarn from a long piece of construction paper rolled into a stick, in order to make a fishing pole with a fish.
5. Students may see a summer fun video or a vacation video.

Learning Styles

Linguistic (hearing stories), spatial (coloring and drawing), interpersonal (working together for ideas), mathematical (thinking logically), and bodily kinesthetic (fishing).

Teaching Team

Art, reading, and library teachers.

Suggested Sources

Borden, Louise. *Abby the Lifeguard.* New York: Scholastic, 1991.
Brown, Marc. *Arthur's Family Vacation.* New York: Random House, 1999. [Video]
Low, Alice. *Summer.* New York: Random House, 2001.
Seuss, Dr. [Theodor Geisel]. *One Fish, Two Fish, Red Fish, Blue Fish.* New York: Random House, 1988.
Waters, Jennifer. *Summer Fun.* Minneapolis, MN: Compass Books, 2002.

Chapter 2

First Grade Lesson Plans

A solid, professionally based library lesson plan is built around the developmental needs of students at their grade level, around the McREL or Kendall and Marzano National Education Language Arts Standards and Benchmarks, the AASL (American Association of School Libraries), and the AECT (Association for Educational Communications and Technology) Information Literacy Standards, and around the various learning styles of students found in Gardner's Multiple Intelligences framework. (The selected AASL/AECT standards and Gardner's Multiple Intelligences fully described in the introduction.) All of the following lessons are built around these standards, benchmarks, and skills in order to ensure that all students appreciate different forms of literature and are competent users of information, and so become information literate.

Each lesson plan includes student objectives, team teaching suggestions, and suggested sources. Furthermore, each lesson is designed to last approximately twenty minutes. All lessons have been field-tested. They provide individual or small-group worksheet work. The lessons are designed to make library learning enjoyable, to be easily accomplished in a librarian's or library teacher's busy schedule, and to be grounded in solid standards and benchmarks. Each lesson has a direct reference to the following McREL standards and benchmarks, as well as a direct reference to the AASL/AECT standards.

First Grade Library Standards and Language Arts Benchmarks (McREL)

Reprinted by permission of McREL

First grade students will be able to:

Use the general skills and strategies of the writing process. (Standard 1)

1. Use writing and other methods (e.g., using letters) to describe. (Standard 1, Benchmark 6)

Gather and use information for research purposes. (Standard 4)

2. Use a variety of sources to gather information (e.g., informational books, pictures, charts, indexes, videos, Internet). (Standard 4, Benchmark 2)
3. Use maps to get information. (Standard 4, Benchmark 6, under grades 3–5)

Use the general skills and strategies of the reading process. (Standard 5)

4. Use meaning clues (e.g., pictures) to aid in comprehension. (Standard 5, Benchmark 2)
5. Use a picture dictionary. (Standard 5, Benchmark 5)
6. Know that books have titles, authors, and often illustrators. (Standard 5, Benchmark 12, under Pre-K)

Use reading skills and strategies to understand and interpret a variety of literary texts. (Standard 6)

7. Use reading skills and strategies to understand a variety of familiar literary text (e.g., fairy tales, folktales, fiction, nonfiction, legends, fables, myths, poems, nursery rhymes, picture books, predictable books). (Standard 6, Benchmark 1)
8. Know the elements that compose a story (e.g., character, plot, events, setting). (Standard 6, Benchmark 2)
9. Know the difference between fact and fiction, real and make-believe.(Standard 6, Benchmark 4)

Use reading skills and strategies to understand and interpret a variety of informational texts. (Standard 7)

10. Use prior knowledge and experience to understand and respond to new information. (Standard 7, Benchmark 6, under grades 3–5)

Use listening and speaking strategies for different purposes. (Standard 8)

11. Create or act out familiar stories, rhymes, and plays. (Standard 8, Benchmark 9)

Fly, Ladybug!

What color is missing from the ladybug? Color it.
Color the wristband and add the ladybug to it.
Watch it fly!

From Joyce Keeling, *Lesson Plans for the Busy Librarian: A Standards Based Approach for the Elementary Library Media Center*, Volume 2. Westport, CT: Libraries Unlimited. © 2006.

Fly, Ladybug!

Standards

Students will

- Use meaning clues (e.g., pictures) to aid in comprehension. (McREL 4)
- Use reading skills and strategies to understand a variety of familiar literary text (e.g. fairy tales, folktales, fiction, nonfiction, legends, fables, myths, poems, nursery rhymes, picture books, predictable books). (McREL 7)
- Know the elements that compose a story (e.g., character, plot, events, setting). (McREL 8)
- Know the difference between fact and fiction, real and make-believe. (McREL 9)
- Create or act out familiar stories, rhymes, and plays. (McREL 11)
- Evaluate information critically and competently. (AASL/AECT 2)
- Participate effectively in groups to pursue and generate information. (AASL/AECT 9)

Objectives

Students hear and see fiction and nonfiction ladybug books, and recognize the differences between fiction and nonfiction. Students list facts, and color and create ladybug wrist puppets.

Directions

1. The library or science teachers read a nonfiction ladybug book
2. Teachers prompt students for some simple ladybug facts and write the suggestions on the board.
3. Teachers read a fiction ladybug book and discuss its plot and character.
4. After being shown the nonfiction and fiction books' illustrations, students explain why each is nonfiction or fiction.
5. Students color and cut out the ladybugs and the wristbands.
6. Teachers help students to attach ladybugs to the center of the wristbands and then attach the ladybug wristbands to their wrists.
7. Students make the ladybugs fly, and perhaps have the bugs act out the fiction plot.

Learning Styles

Linguistic (reading and discussing), spatial (coloring), interpersonal (group discussion), and bodily kinesthetic (flying ladybugs).

Teaching Team

Library and science teachers.

Suggested Resources

Brown, Ruth. *Ladybug, Ladybug*. New York: Dutton, 1992. [Fiction]
Carle, Eric. *The Grouchy Ladybug*. New York: HarperCollins, 1996. [Fiction]
Coughlan, Cheryl. *Lady Bugs*. Mankato, MN: Pebble Books, 1990. [Nonfiction]
Himmelman, John. *A Ladybug's Life*. Chicago, IL: Children's Press, 1998. [Nonfiction]

Vote on Your Caldecott Book

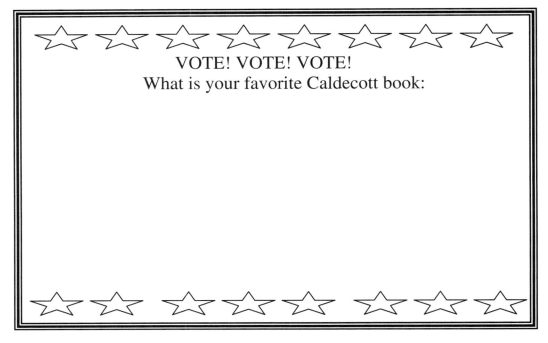

VOTE! VOTE! VOTE!
What is your favorite Caldecott book:

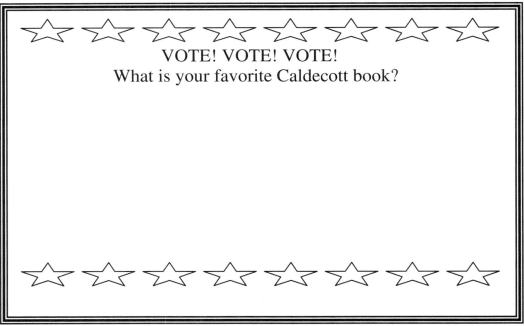

VOTE! VOTE! VOTE!
What is your favorite Caldecott book?

From Joyce Keeling, *Lesson Plans for the Busy Librarian: A Standards Based Approach for the Elementary Library Media Center*, Volume 2. Westport, CT: Libraries Unlimited. © 2006.

Vote on Your Caldecott Book

Standards

Students will

- Use meaning clues (e.g., pictures) to aid in comprehension. (McREL 4)
- Know that books have titles, authors, and often illustrators. (McREL 6)
- Use reading skills and strategies to understand a variety of familiar literary text (e.g., fairy tales, folktales, fiction, nonfiction, legends, fables, myths, poems, nursery rhymes, picture books, predictable books). (McREL 7)
- Appreciate and enjoy literature and other creative expressions of information. (AASL/AECT 5)

Objectives

Students hear, see, and vote on Caldecott books. They review title, author, and illustrator.

Directions

1. The library teacher decorates a voting box for the ballots from the students' worksheets (each worksheet has ballots for two students).
2. The library and reading teachers show the illustrations and read at least two or three Caldecott books. Titles, authors, and illustrators are also discussed.
3. Teachers list the titles they have read to the students on the board.
4. Students vote for their favorite Caldecott title by writing and illustrating it on their ballot.
5. Ballots are put in the box, then counted.
6. The class's winning Caldecott book is displayed.

Learning Styles

Linguistic (seeing pictures, writing), spatial (drawing), and intrapersonal (voting).

Teaching Team

Library and reading teachers.

Suggested Resources

Cronin, Doreen. *Click, Clack Moo: Cows That Type*. New York: Simon & Schuster, 2000.
Falconer, Ian. *Olivia*. New York: Atheneum, 2000.
Rylant, Cynthia. *Relatives Came*. New York: Aladdin, 1985.
Sendak, Maurice. *Where the Wild Things Are*. New York: HarperCollins, 1991.
Simont, Marc. *Stray Dog*. New York: HarperCollins, 1988.
Stevens, Janet. *Tops and Bottoms*. New York: Harcourt Brace, 1995.
Taback, Simms. *Joseph Had a Little Overcoat*. New York: Viking, 1999.
Willems, Mo. *Don't Let the Pigeon Drive the Bus*! New York: Hyperion, 2003.
List of all Caldecott Award–winning books at http://www.ala.org/alsc/caldecott.html

Ocean Creatures

This ocean needs some animals. Using nonfiction books, find the right colors for the ocean animals. Color everything. Put the animals back into the water.

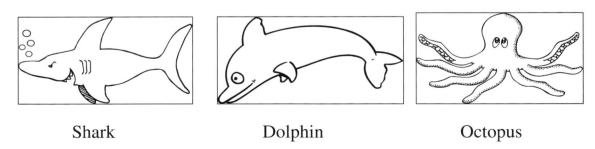

Shark   Dolphin   Octopus

From Joyce Keeling, *Lesson Plans for the Busy Librarian: A Standards Based Approach for the Elementary Library Media Center*, Volume 2. Westport, CT: Libraries Unlimited. © 2006.

Ocean Creatures

Standards

Students will

- Use a variety of sources to gather information (e.g., informational books, pictures, charts, indexes, videos, Internet). (McREL 2)
- Use meaning clues (e.g., pictures) to aid in comprehension. (McREL 4)
- Access information efficiently and effectively. (AASL/AECT 1)
- Evaluate information critically and competently. (AASL/AECT 2)
- Use information effectively and creatively. (AASL/AECT 3)
- Strive for excellence in information seeking and knowledge. (AASL/AECT 6)
- Recognize the importance of information to a democratic society. (AASL/AECT 7)
- Participate effectively in groups to pursue and generate information. (AASL/AECT 9)

Objectives

Students research facts and colors of dolphins, sharks, and the octopus. They color the animals and the ocean, and put the animals back into the ocean.

Directions

1. The library teacher gives small student groups encyclopedias and books containing information on dolphins, octopi, and sharks, and guides them in finding pictures and/or print facts about these animals.
2. The science teacher has the groups share their facts with the class.
3. Students find the natural animal coloring and then color the worksheet animals using the correct colors. Students color the ocean scene.
4. Students cut out and glue the animals on the ocean. Students write 2–3 facts they have found about the animals on the back of the worksheet.

Learning Styles

Linguistic (reading, discussing), spatial (coloring), interpersonal (group work), and intrapersonal (working alone).

Teaching Team

Library and science teachers.

Suggested Resources

Cooper, Jason. *Large Sea Creatures*. Vero Beach, Florida: Rourke, 1992.
Cooper, Jason. *Small Sea Creatures*. Vero Beach, Florida: Rourke, 1992.
Gunzi, Christiane. *The Best Book of Sharks*. New York: Kingfisher, 2001.
Kite, Patricia. *The Octopus*. Morton Grove, IL: Albert Whitman, 1995.
Rustad, Martha E. H. *Dolphins*. Mankato, MN: Capstone Press, 2001.
World Book. *World Book Encyclopedia*. Chicago, IL: 2004.

Putting Things in Order

Color the following pictures about school. Cut out the squares. Put them in the right ABC order. Finally, color the cover and put it in front. You have started your little Picture Dictionary! Keep adding pages.

Colors

Bus

My
Picture
Dictionary

ABC

By:_____

Apple

From Joyce Keeling, *Lesson Plans for the Busy Librarian: A Standards Based Approach for the Elementary Library Media Center*, Volume 2. Westport, CT: Libraries Unlimited. © 2006.

Putting Things in Order

Standards

Students will

- Use meaning clues (e.g. pictures) to aid in comprehension. (McREL 4)
- Use a picture dictionary. (McREL 5).
- Access information efficiently and effectively. (AASL/AECT 1)
- Use information effectively and creatively. (AASL/AECT 3)
- Pursue information related to personal interests. (AASL/AECT 4)
- Strive for excellence in information seeking and knowledge generation. (AASL/AECT 6)

Objectives

Students learn how to use picture dictionaries. Students color and make their own picture dictionary.

Directions

1. The language arts and library teachers show pages of actual picture dictionaries and explain how the dictionaries work.
2. Students color the worksheet squares for their picture dictionary. Simple picture dictionaries often have pages by themes, so this dictionary has a school theme.
3. Students cut out the squares and put them in ABC order.
4. Teachers check to make for sure the pages are in correct ABC order and help students put on the cover and staple the book pages together.
5. In the remaining time, small groups of students read picture dictionaries as the teachers check that they are using the dictionaries correctly.
6. In their regular classroom, students may keep adding and drawing their own ABC pages of school things to their booklets until they have completed the dictionaries.

Learning Styles

Linguistic (reading), spatial (coloring), interpersonal (group work), mathematical (thinking logically), and intrapersonal (working alone).

Teaching Team

Library and language arts teachers.

Suggested Sources

Cote, Pamela. *My Big Dictionary*. Boston, MA: Houghton Mifflin, 1994.

Morales, Roberta Collier. *The American Heritage Picture Dictionary*. Boston, MA: Houghton Mifflin, 2001.

Weinberger, Kimberly and Gina Shaw. *Hello Reader!* New York: Scholastic, 1999.

Wilkes, Angela. *English Picture Dictionary*. New York: Passport Books, 1986.

Pilgrims

The pilgrims are getting ready for Thanksgiving dinner.

1. What will the boy do with his wood? He will _____

_____

2. What will the girl do with her wheat? She will _____

_____

Pilgrims

Standards

Students will

- Use writing and other methods (e.g., using letters) to describe. (McREL 1)
- Use a variety of sources to gather information (e.g., informational books, pictures, charts, indexes, videos, Internet). (McREL 2)
- Use meaning clues (e.g., pictures) to aid in comprehension. McREL 4)
- Use reading skills and strategies to understand a variety of familiar literary text forms (e.g., fairy tales, folktales, fiction, nonfiction, legends, fables, myths, poems, nursery rhymes, picture books, predictable books). (McREL 7)
- Evaluate information critically and competently. (AASL/AECT 2)
- Recognize the importance of information to a democratic society. (AASL/AECT 7)

Objectives

Students hear, see, and discuss books or a video about pilgrims and how they lived and worked. They color the paper-doll pilgrims and answer the questions.

Directions

1. The social studies or library teacher reads one or two books on the pilgrims' lifestyle and work. A video may be shown as well.
2. Students tell what they saw and heard about pilgrim life and work.
3. On the worksheets, students write what the pilgrim boy could make from wood for Thanksgiving (e.g., tables), and what the girl could make from wheat (e.g., bread).
4. The pilgrim figures are colored and are either used as paper dolls to act out a Thanksgiving celebration, or put into a student-drawn Thanksgiving scene.

Learning Styles

Linguistic (writing), spatial (coloring, writing), bodily kinesthetic (acting), interpersonal (working alone), and mathematical (thinking logically).

Teaching Team

Library and social studies teachers.

Suggested Sources

Kendall, Russ. *On the Mayflower: Voyage of the Ship's Apprentice.* New York: Scholastic, 1996.
Waters, Kate. *Sarah Morton's Day: A Day in the Life of a Pilgrim Girl.* New York: Scholastic, 1989.
Waters, Kate. *Samuel Eaton's Day: A Day in the Life of a Pilgrim Boy.* New York: Scholastic, 1993.
Weston Woods. *The Pilgrims of Plymouth.* Westport, CT: Weston Woods, 1998. [Video]

Dog Bones

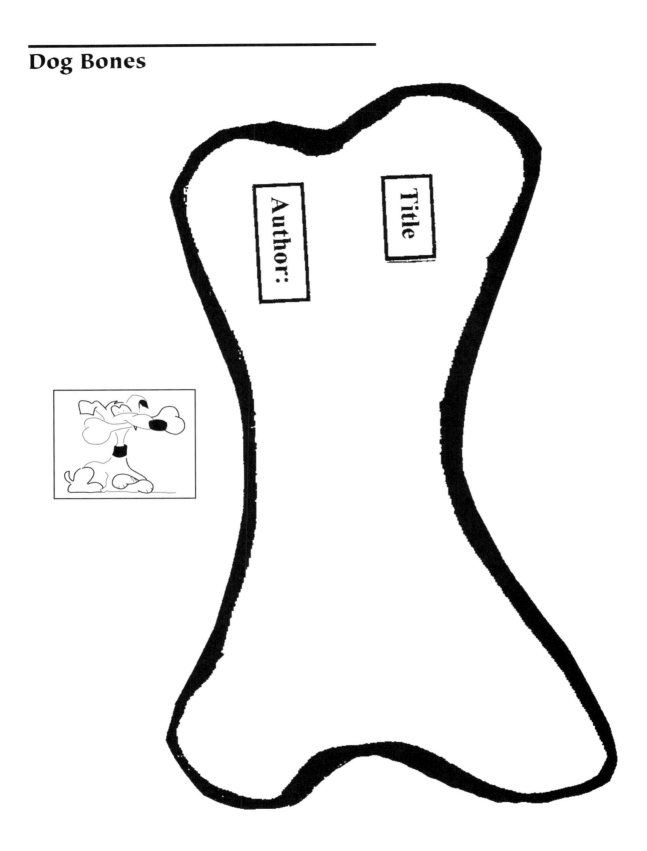

Author:

Title

Dog Bones

Standards

Students will

- Use writing and other methods to describe. (McREL 1)
- Use meaning clues (e.g. pictures) to aid in comprehension. (McREL 4)
- Know that books have titles, authors, and often illustrators. (McREL 6)
- Know the elements that composes a story (e.g. character, plot, events, setting). (McREL 8)
- Use prior knowledge and experience to understand and respond to new information. (McREL 10)
- Appreciate and enjoy literature and other creative expressions. (AASL/AECT 5)
- Participate effectively in groups to pursue and generate information. (AASL/AECT 9)

Objectives

Students hear various fictional dog books and discuss plots and characters. They also review and write the title and author.

Directions

1. The library and reading teachers choose two or three fictional dog books and writes the title and author of each book on the board before students arrive.
2. After pointing out each title, author, and illustrator, the library and reading teachers read the fictional dog books.
3. After hearing the books, students discuss main plot and characters.
4. On their dog bones, students write the title and author of their favorite dog book that they heard.
5. Students lightly color and then cut out the bones.

Learning Styles

Linguistic (hearing stories, writing), spatial (coloring), interpersonal (working alone), and intrapersonal (group work).

Teaching Team

Reading and library teachers.

Suggested Sources

Capucilli, Alyssa Satin. *Biscuit*. New York: HarperCollins, 2000. [Fiction]
Inkpen, Mick. *Kipper's Snowy Day*. New York: Harcourt Brace, 1996. [Fiction]
Kellogg, Steven. *A Penguin Pup for Pinkerton*. New York: Dial, 2001. [Fiction]
Provenson, Alice. *A Day in the Life of Murphy*. New York: Scholastic, 2004. [Fiction]
Simont, Marc. *Stray Dog*. New York: HarperCollins, 2004. [Fiction]
Zion, Gene. *Harry the Dirty Dog*. New York: HarperCollins, 1984 [Fiction]

Library Game Time

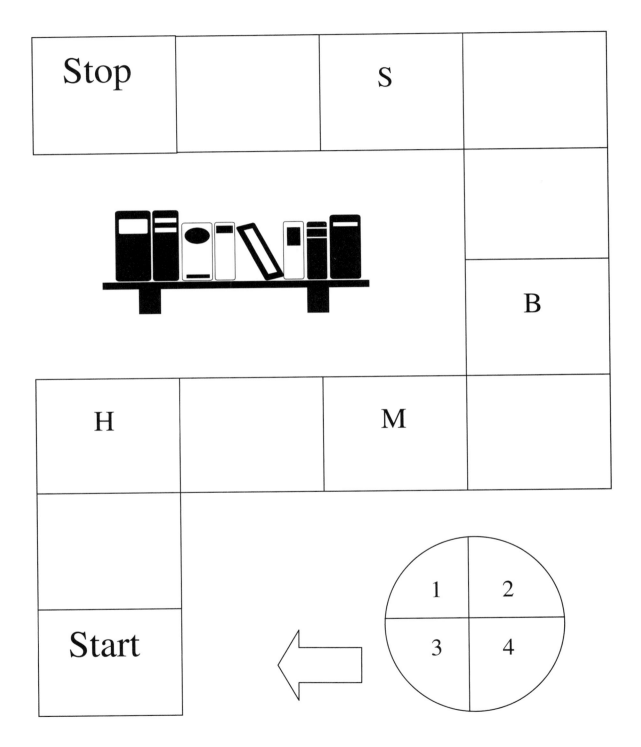

From Joyce Keeling, *Lesson Plans for the Busy Librarian: A Standards Based Approach for the Elementary Library Media Center*, Volume 2. Westport, CT: Libraries Unlimited. © 2006.

Play the Library Game! (Library Game Time)

Standards

Students will

- Know that books have titles, authors, and often illustrators. (McREL 6)
- Use prior knowledge and experience to understand and respond to new information. (McREL 10)
- Access information efficiently and effectively. (AASL/AECT 1)
- Strive for excellence in information seeking and knowledge generation. (AASL/AECT 6)

Objectives

Students learn that fiction books in the library are in alphabetical order as they play the library game.

Directions

1. Copy the student worksheet onto cardstock or stiff paper. Cut out the game arrows and attach them with a brad paper fastener to the middle of the circle on the students' activity papers before class.
2. Library and reading teachers show students that easy-reading fiction books are in alphabetical order (ABC order) on the shelf and give many examples.
3. Teachers read an ABC book, then show that it is shelved by the author's last name in ABC order.
4. Students create a game marker by tearing a small corner off from their game sheets and coloring it.
5. Students are ready to play! They take turns to spin the arrow and move their game pieces the number of places shown. If they land on a letter, they find a book with that call letter and bring it to their table. Teachers check that the book and game letter match. Then the next student plays. They play until one reaches the finish line!
6. Students may check out one of the books, and finally all line up together in ABC order.

Learning Styles

Linguistic (hearing/discussing), mathematical (being challenged), bodily kinesthetic (playing games), and interpersonal (working together).

Teaching Team

Library and reading teachers.

Suggested Sources

Dodd, Emma. *Dog's ABC*. New York: Dutton, 2002.
Holly, Hobbie. *Toot & Puddle's ABC*. Boston: Little and Brown, 2000.
Pfister, Marcus. *Rainbow Fish A, B, C*. New York: North-South Books, 2002.
Sobel, Jane. *B is for Bulldozer*. New York: Harcourt Brace, 2003.

Christmas Letters

Write a letter!

Dear _____,

_____

_____

_____

_____

_____

From,

_____

Christmas Letters

Standards

Students will

- Use writing and other strategies of the writing process. (McREL 1)
- Know books have titles, authors, and often illustrators. (McREL 6)
- Know the elements that composes a story (e.g. character, plot, events, setting). (McReL 8)
- Appreciate and enjoy literature. (AASL/AECT 5)
- Strive for excellence in information seeking and knowledge generation. (AASL/AECT 6)

Objectives

Students hear and discuss a book about Christmas and mailing letters. Students then write a very brief Christmas letter explaining the plot of the story.

Directions

1. The library teacher reads a fictional book on mailing something or writing a letter, and Christmas. Title, author, illustrator, and plot will be discussed.
2. The language arts teacher leads students in writing a very simple Christmas letter to someone. They are encouraged to write about the story plot.
3. The library and language arts teachers encourage students to write their best as they monitor student writing.
4. Students color around their letters to give the letters a festive look.
5. Students are encouraged to give their Christmas letters away.

Learning Styles

Linguistic (writing), spatial (coloring), and intrapersonal (working alone).

Teaching Team

Library and language arts teachers.

Suggested Sources

Ahlberg, Janet and Allan. *The Jolly Christmas Postman.* New York: Scholastic, 1996. [Fiction]
Holabird, Katherine. *Angelina's Christmas.* New York: Clarkson N. Potter, 1985. [Fiction]
Stock, Catherine. *Christmas Time.* New York: Bradbury, 1990. [Fiction]

Mitten Time?

When is it time to wear mittens? Color the pictures and mitten. Cut out the words and glue them on the correct pictures. Attach the mitten to the circle.

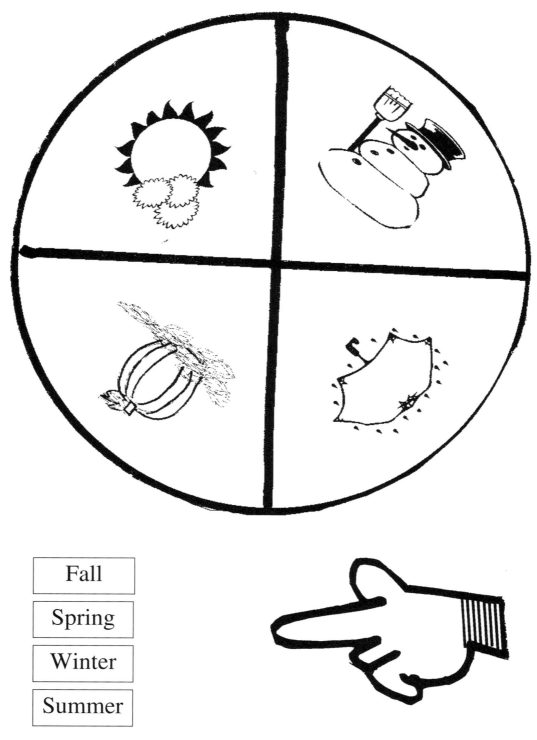

Fall

Spring

Winter

Summer

Mitten Time?

Standards

Students will

- Use writing and other methods (e.g. using letters) to describe. (McREL 1)
- Use meaning clues (e.g. pictures) to aid in comprehension. (McREL 4)
- Use prior knowledge and experience to understand and respond to new information. (McREL 10)
- Evaluate information critically and competently. (AASL/AECT 2)
- Use information effectively and creatively. (AASL/AECT3)
- Participate effectively in groups to pursue and generate information. (AASL/AECT 9)

Objectives

Students hear and discuss season books. Students color and create a seasons' wheel in order to answer questions about seasons.

Directions

1. Each library and science teacher reads a book about seasons.
2. The science teacher discusses the books asking students seasonal questions. For example, what happens in the fall, and so on.
3. Students color the pictures on the wheel and color the mitten.
4. Students cut out the season titles and glue them on the wheel.
5. The mitten is fastened with a paper fastener to the wheel.
6. The teachers ask season questions as students place the mitten on the appropriate seasonal place on the wheel.
7. The library teacher may read a mitten book.

Learning Styles

Linguistic (hearing facts and then stories), mathematical (thinking logically), spatial (coloring), and intrapersonal (working alone).

Teaching Team

Library and science teachers.

Suggested Sources

Bennett, Davie. *Seasons*. New York; Readers Digest Kids, 1988.

Borden, Louise. *Caps, Socks and Mittens*. A Book About The Four Seasons. New York: Scholastic, 1989. [Nonfiction]

Brett, Jan. *The Mitten: A Ukrainian Folktale*. New York: Putnam, 1989 [Fiction]

Maas, Robert. *When Winter Comes*. New York; Holt, 1993. [Fiction]

Saunders-Smith, Gail. *Warm Clothes*. Mankato, MN: Capstone, 1998. [Fiction]

Thayer, Tanya. *Winter*. Minneapolis, MN: Lerner, 2002. [Nonfiction]

Tresselt, Alvin. *The Mitten*. New York: Mulberry Press, 1989. [Fiction]

Getting Better!

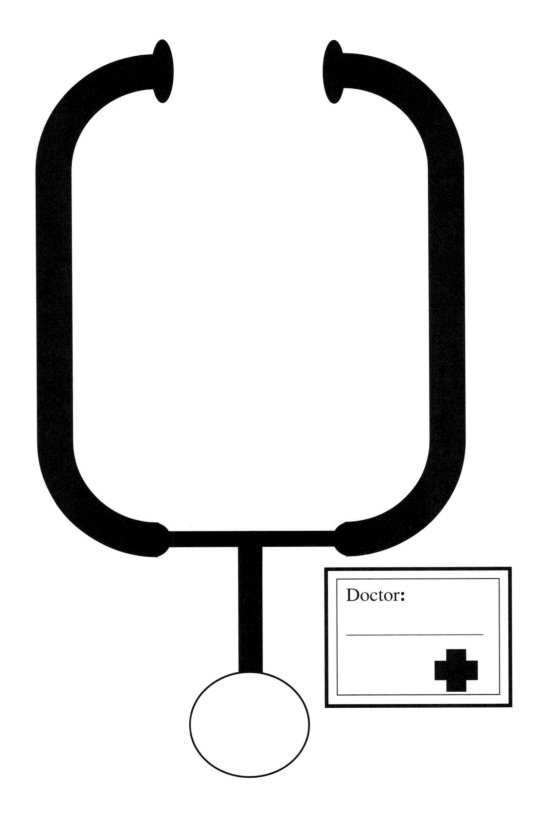

Doctor:

Getting Better!

Standards

Students will

- Use writing and other methods (e.g., using letters) to describe. (McREL 1)
- Use a variety of sources to gather information (e.g., informational books, pictures, charts, indexes, videos, Internet). (McREL 2)
- Use meaning clues (e.g., pictures) to aid in comprehension. (McREL 4)
- Evaluate information critically and competently. (AASL/AECT 2)
- Use information effectively and creatively. (AASL/AECT 3)
- Pursue information related to personal interests. (AASL/AECT 4)

Objectives

Students hear stories and discuss simple facts about a doctor's career. They write a fact. They hear and discuss a fiction book on doctors or medicine. They cut out and wear medical badges and a stethoscope.

Directions

1. Copy student sheets onto cardstock or stiff paper.
2. The library teacher reads a simple nonfiction book about doctors.
3. The science teacher discusses the book and writes a couple of facts on the board
4. Students write a fact inside the worksheet stethoscopes.
5. Students hear a fiction book on medicine or see a video, and then discuss it briefly.
6. Students write their names on the medical badges, and tape them on their shirts.
7. If desired, students use the stethoscope to act out what they saw and heard.

Learning Styles

Linguistic (hearing facts, writing), mathematical (thinking logically), interpersonal (discussing), spatial (imaging), and bodily kinesthetic (acting).

Teaching Team

Science and library teachers.

Suggested Sources

London, Jonathan. *Froggy Goes to the Doctor.* New York: Penguin, 2002. [Fiction]
Owen, Ann. *Keeping You Healthy: A Book about Doctors.* Minneapolis, MN: Picture Window Books, 2004. [Nonfiction]
Rey, Margaret. *Curious George Goes to the Hospital.* Boston: HoughtonMifflin, 1993. [Fiction]
Schaefer, Lola. *We Need Doctors.* Mankato, MN: Capstone, 2000. [Nonfiction]
Steig, William. *Doctor DeSoto.* Norwalk, CT: Weston Woods, 1984. [Video]
World Book. *Childcraft How and Why Library.* Chicago, IL: World Book, 2004.

Jack and the Giant

Jack and the Giant

Standards

Students will

- Use reading skills and strategies to understand a variety of familiar literary text (e.g., fairy tales, folktales, fiction, nonfiction, legends, fables, myths, poems, nursery rhymes, picture books, predictable books). (McREL 7)
- Know the elements that compose a story (e.g., character, plot, events, setting). (McREL 8)
- Create or act out familiar stories, rhymes, and plays. (McREL 11)
- Appreciate and enjoy literature and other creative expressions. (AASL/AECT 5)
- Strive for excellence in information seeking and knowledge generation. (AASL/AECT 6)

Objectives

Students hear a fairy tale and discuss its plot, setting, characters, and events. Students make puppets and act out the story.

Directions

1. Copy student sheets onto sturdy paper for making puppets.
2. The library teacher reads *Jack and the Beanstalk* and tells why the story is a fairy tale (it involves magic, and so on).
3. The reading teacher discusses story events, characters, plots, and setting.
4. Students color and cut out the worksheet figures of the giant, Jack, and the beanstalk.
5. The art teacher helps students make puppets. Plastic straws are fastened to the giant and Jack puppets. A background is created with the beanstalk.
6. Students act out the story while the library and reading teachers listen to and watch the puppet play for story comprehension.

Learning Styles

Linguistic (reading, discussing), spatial (coloring), bodily kinesthetic (acting), and intrapersonal (creating puppets).

Teaching Team

Art, library, and reading teachers.

Suggested Sources

Beer, Barbara Vagnozzi. *Jack and the Beanstalk.* Spain: Child's Play, 2004.
Kellogg, Steven. *Jack and the Beanstalk.* New York: Morrow, 1991.
Lorenz, Albert. *Jack and the Beanstalk: How a Small Fellow Solved a Big Problem.* New York: Harry A. Abrams, 2002.
Moore, Maggie. *Jack and the Beanstalk.* Minneapolis, MN: Picture Window Books, 2003.

Birthday Times Bring Birthday Rhymes!

Write a birthday rhyme on the cake.

Birthday Times Bring Birthday Rhymes!

Standards

Students will

- Use writing and other methods to describe. (McREL 1)
- Use reading skills and strategies to understand a variety of familiar literary text (e.g., fairy tales, folktales, fiction, nonfiction, legends, fables, myths, poems, nursery rhymes, picture books, predictable books). (McREL 7)
- Appreciate and enjoy literature and other creative expressions. (AASL/AECT 5)
- Participate effectively in groups to pursue and generate information. (AASL/AECT 9)

Objectives

Students hear birthday rhymes or silly rhymes. They become familiar with one rhyme and write it.

Directions

1. The reading and library teacher read several fairly short birthday rhymes and/or other rhymes.
2. The class chooses a favorite rhyme and the teacher writes it on the board.
3. Students repeat the board rhyme several times
4. Students write the board rhyme on their birthday cakes.
5. The cakes are colored.

Learning Styles

Linguistic (writing), spatial (coloring), musical (rhymes), and intrapersonal (writing and reciting a rhyme).

Teaching Team

Library and reading teachers.

Suggested Sources

Goldstein, Bobbye S. *Birthday Rhymes, Special Times*. New York: Doubleday, 1993.
Prelutsly, Jack. *Read-Aloud Rhymes for the Very Young*. New York: Alfred A. Knopf, 1986.
Resnick, James P. *The Classic Treasury of Silly Poetry*. Philadelphia: Running Press Book Publications, 1995.
Robinson, Fay. *A Frog Inside My Hat*. Mahwah, NJ: Troll, 1993. [Birthday rhymes]

Racing Math

Get your car. Start Racing! Stop to answer the math problems. Will you win?

Get Ready! Get Set! Go!

Racer 1 Start Here   Racer 2 Start Here

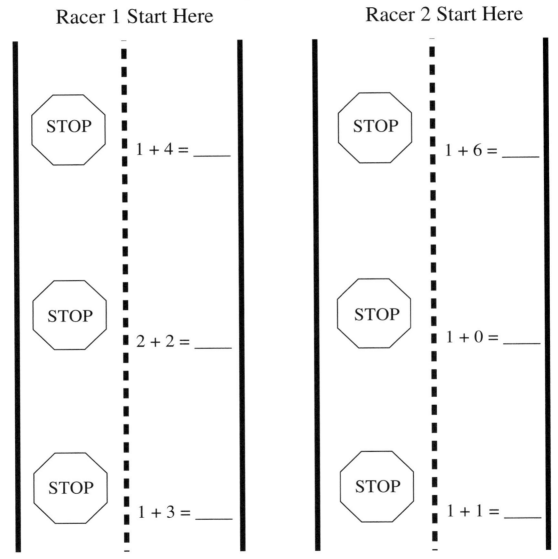

STOP   1 + 4 = ____

STOP   2 + 2 = ____

STOP   1 + 3 = ____

STOP   1 + 6 = ____

STOP   1 + 0 = ____

STOP   1 + 1 = ____

Stop! You Won!

Racing Math

Standards

Students will

- Use meaning clues (e.g., pictures) to aid in comprehension. (McREL 4)
- Know books have titles, authors, and often illustrators. (McREL 6)
- Use prior knowledge and experience to understand and respond to new information. (McREL 10)
- Appreciate and enjoy literature and other creative expression. (AASL/AECT 5)

Objectives

Students hear and recite addition and subtraction facts from library books. Students review title, author, and illustrator. Student pairs play a math game.

Directions

1. The library teacher reads some books about addition and subtraction after pointing out the titles, authors, and illustrators.
2. Students complete math problems from the books.
3. Each student colors and cuts out one worksheet racecar.
4. The math teacher matches student pairs. Paired students race against each other by taking turns giving addition answers orally. If the correct answer is given, the racer moves on. until a student reaches the racetrack end. Teachers monitor for understanding.
5. The racing game is played a few times, each time with new student pairs.
6. If time, students read other library math books or play an online math game.

Learning Styles

Linguistic (hearing math books), mathematical (simple math), spatial (coloring), intrapersonal (completing math facts), and interpersonal (working in groups).

Teaching Team

Library and math teachers.

Suggested Sources

Curry, Don L. *More Bugs? Less Bugs?* Mankato, MN: Capstone, 2000.
Gray, Catherine. *One, Two, and Four No More?* Boston: Houghton, Mifflin, 1988.
Harshman, Marc. *Only One.* New York: Cobble Hill Books, 1992.
Maccarone, Grace. *Monster Math.* New York: Scholastic, 1998.
Sierra, Judy. *Counting Crocodiles.* New York: Scholastic, 1998.
Online math games for primary students:
http://www.funbrain.com/math
http://www.primarygames.com/math

The Cat and the Bell

Color the cat and the bell.

Belling the Cat was trying to get all the mice. They were not safe from the cat. The mice called a meeting. They said someone should put a bell around the neck of Belling the Cat. But who would do it? It had to be someone who was really brave! Will it be you?

The Cat and the Bell

Standards

Students will

- Use reading skills and strategies to understand a variety of familiar literary text (e.g. fairy tales, folktales, fiction, nonfiction, legends, fables, myths, poems, nursery rhymes, picture books, predictable book). (McREL 7)
- Know the elements that compose a story (e.g. character, plot, events, setting). (McREL 8)
- Use prior knowledge and experience to understand and respond to new information. (McREL 10)
- Appreciate and enjoy literature and other creative expressions. (AASL/AECT 5)
- Participate effectively in groups to pursue and generate information. (AASL/AECT 9)

Objectives

Students show that they understand the elements of fables, and they hear a fable. They review setting, character, events, and main plot. Students color their worksheets.

Directions

1. The library or reading teacher reads the "Cat and the Bell" fable. Teachers define the elements of fables (fables have a moral, animals usually talk, and so on)
2. Setting, characters, events, and main plot are discussed. Students are asked whether they would change the story in any way.
3. Students color the cat and the bell.
4. Teachers read the summary of the story on student worksheets and ask students whether they would be brave like the mouse?
5. Students cut out the bell and place it on the cat's neck to prove that they are brave!
6. If there is time, students may hear and discuss other fables.

Learning Styles

Linguistic (hearing), spatial (coloring), interpersonal (group discussion), and intrapersonal (working alone).

Teaching Team

Library and reading teachers.

Suggested Sources

Daily, Don. "The Cat and the Bell." *The Classic Treasury of Aesop's Fables*. Philadelphia, PA: Courage Books, 1999.
Paxton, Tom. *Belling the Cat and Other Aesop's Fables*. New York: Harper Collins, 1990.
Pinkney, Jerry. "Belling the Cat." *Aesop's Fables*. New York: Seastar Books, 2000.

A Valentine Gift

A Valentine's Day Note:

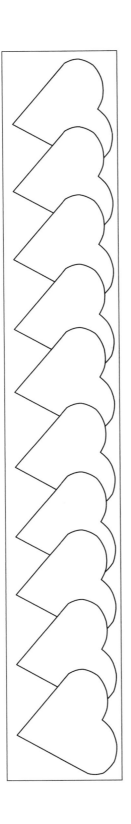

Valentine's Day is a time
to share something of mine.
Here is a gift that I hope is fine.
Please be my Valentine!

A Valentine Gift

Standards

Students will

- Know that books have titles, authors, and often illustrators. (McREL 6)
- Use reading skills and strategies to understand a variety of familiar literary text (e.g. fairy tales, folktales, fiction, nonfiction, legends, fables, myths, poems, nursery rhymes, picture books, predictable books). (McREL 7)
- Know the elements that composes a book (e.g. character, plot, events, setting). (McREL 8)
- Participate effectively in groups to pursue and generate information. (AASL/AECT 9)

Objectives

Students hear and discuss Valentine stories and review the author, title, illustrator, shelf location, and plot. They color and create a heart bracelet with a rhyming card.

Directions

1. The library teacher reads two Valentine books that mention hearts. Title, author, illustrator, plot, and shelf location are also discussed.
2. Students color the hearts on their sheets.
3. Students make a heart bracelet from the long worksheet heart strip. The strip is cut out, and the ends are taped together. The bracelet is a gift.
4. The reading teacher helps students create a class rhyme to go with the bracelet. Ideas may be found from a rhyme book. The worksheet rhyme may also be used. The rhyme is written on the note, and it is then cut out.
5. Students recite their rhymes. Bracelets and notes will be given away.

Learning Styles

Linguistic (hearing stories and writing), spatial (coloring and creating), musical (rhythm), interpersonal (discussing, giving), and intrapersonal (working alone).

Teaching Team

Library and reading teachers.

Suggested Sources

Hoban, Lillian. *Silly Tilly's Valentine*. New York: HarperTrophy, 1998. [Fiction]
McMullan, Kate. *Fluffy's Valentine's Day*. New York: Scholastic, 1998. [Fiction]
Roop, Peter. *Let's Celebrate Valentine's Day*. New York: Millbrook Press, 1999. [Rhymes]
Scull, Robert. *Happy Valentine's Day!* New York: Simon, 2002. [Fiction]
Shannon, George. *Heart to Heart*. Boston, MA: Houghton Mifflin, 1995. [Fiction]
Watson, Wendy. *Valentine Foxes*. New York: Franklin Watts, 1989. [Fiction]

The Princess and the Pea

A Bed

Mattresses

A Princess

What do mattresses, a bed, and a pea have to do with a princess?

Pea

The Princess and the Pea

Standards

Students will

- Use reading skills and strategies to understand a variety of familiar literary text (e.g. fairy tales, folktales, fiction, nonfiction, legends, fables, myths, poems, nursery rhymes, picture books, predictable books). (McREL 7)
- Know the elements that compose a story (e.g. character, plot, events, setting). (McREL 8)
- Create or act out familiar stories, rhymes, and plays. (McREL 11)
- Appreciate and enjoy literature in information seeking and knowledge generation. (AASL/ AECT 6)
- Participate effectively in groups to pursue and generate information. (AASL/AECT 9)

Objectives

Students hear a fairy tale and discuss its plot, characters, setting, and events. They color and create an interactive scene.

Directions

1. The library or reading teacher reads "The Princess and the Pea." Students explain plot, characters, setting, events, and why it's a fairy tale.
2. The teacher reads the worksheet question. Students color the worksheets.
3. Students cut out the worksheet objects, including the question, and use them to create an interactive scene. On a blank piece of colored paper, students glue only the bed and the question.
4. Students enjoy this interactive scene as they use it to actively tell the story and answer the question by putting the pea on top of the bed, adding mattresses, and then adding the princess.

Learning Styles

Linguistic (reading and discussing), spatial (coloring and creating), interpersonal (explaining), intrapersonal (working alone), and bodily kinesthetic (acting).

Teaching Team

Library and reading teacher.

Suggested Sources

Blackaby, Susan. *The Princess and the Pea.* Minneapolis, MN: Picture Window Books, 2003.
Martin, Annie-Claude. "The Princess and the Pea." In *A Treasury of Fairy Tales.* Oxfordshire, England: Transedition Books, 1995.
Ziefert, Harriet. *The Princess and the Pea.* New York: Puffin, 1996.

Mapping

Maps are read by looking at the letters and the numbers together.
The letters and numbers together are called **coordinates**.
Color the objects only when you hear its coordinates.

	A	B	C	D	E
1		◯		☆	
2				♡	△
3	⬡		☾		
4		◯		▭	

Mapping

Standards

Students will

- Use maps to get information. (McREL 3)
- Pursue information related to personal interests. (AASL/AECT 4)
- Strive for excellence in information seeking and knowledge generation. (AASL/AECT 6)
- Recognize the importance of information to a democratic society. (AASL/AECT 7)

Objectives

Students learn how to read map coordinates by using them to locate objects to color on their worksheets.

Directions

1. The library and social studies teachers read the definition of coordinates on the student worksheet and explain how map coordinates are used.

2. Students color the map objects as instructed by one of the teachers, who calls out the coordinates and the color choices while the other teacher checks for learning.

3. In the remaining time, students look at library atlases.

Learning Styles

Linguistic (hearing), mathematical (thinking logically), spatial (coloring, mapping), and intrapersonal (working alone).

Teaching Team

Library and social studies teachers.

Suggested Sources

Any available atlases.

Sheep, Sheep

Sheep, Sheep! Where will you go? What will you do?

Sheep are in a book.
Sheep, will take a look.
Sheep, now where will you be?
Sheep! In the library with me? Oh!

From Joyce Keeling, *Lesson Plans for the Busy Librarian: A Standards Based Approach for the Elementary Library Media Center*, Volume 2. Westport, CT: Libraries Unlimited. © 2006.

Sheep, Sheep

Standards

Students will

- Know books have titles, authors, and often illustrators. (McREL 6)
- Use reading skills and strategies to understand a variety of familiar literary text (e.g., fairy tales, folktales, fiction, nonfiction, legends, fables, myths, poems, nursery rhymes, picture books, predictable books). (McREL 7)
- Know the elements that compose a story (e.g., plot). (McREL 8)
- Appreciate and enjoy literature and other creative expression. (AASL/AECT 5)
- Participate effectively in groups to pursue and generate information. (AASL/AECT 9)

Objectives

Students learn about an author as they hear two of his or her books. They discuss title, author, illustrator and plot, and predict what the stories are about. They color worksheets and repeat the sheep rhyme.

Directions

1. Library and/or reading teachers choose an author who features sheep in one of his or her books, read that book, and then read another book by the same author for an author study. For example, students may hear and see the sheep book and one other book written by either McPhail or by Shaw. Author, title, and illustrator are also discussed.
2. As the teachers are reading, students will make predictions.
3. Book plots are discussed, followed by discussions on how this author's two books are alike and how they are different.
4. Then the library teacher asks students what would happen if a sheep visited the library. Student worksheets are read. Students design a library or book-related background on their worksheets, and then finish by coloring them.
5. Students repeat the sheep rhyme until familiar with it.

Learning Styles

Linguistic (hearing books, discussing), spatial (coloring), musical (rhyming), and interpersonal (group discussions).

Teaching Team

Library and reading teachers.

Suggested Sources

McPhail, David. *The Day the Sheep Showed Up*. New York: Scholastic, 1998.
McPhail, David. *Farm Morning*. New York: Harcourt Brace, 1985.
Shaw, Nancy. *Raccoon Tune*. New York: Henry Holt, 2003.
Shaw, Nancy. *Sheep in a Jeep*. Boston: Houghton Mifflin, 1986.
Shaw, Nancy. *Sheep in a Shop*. Boston: Houghton Mifflin, 1991.

Bunnies and Rabbits

Bunnies and Rabbits

Standards

Students will

- Use a variety of information for research purposes (e.g., informational books, pictures, charts, indexes, videos, Internet). (McREL 2)
- Use meaning clue (e.g., pictures) to aid in comprehension. (McREL 4)
- Know the difference between fact and fiction, reality and make-believe. (McREL 9)
- Evaluate information critically and competently. (AASL/AECT 2)
- Recognize the importance of information to a democratic society. (AASL/AECT 7)

Objectives

Students hear and compare nonfiction and fiction rabbit or bunny sources. They color a rabbit mask and then hop "The Bunny Hop."

Directions

1. Copy student worksheet masks onto stiff paper or cardstock paper.
2. The science teacher reads and discusses rabbit facts from a nonfiction source.
3. The library teacher reads a fiction book featuring rabbits. Then teachers compare book illustrations to discuss what makes the two books fiction or nonfiction.
4. Students color and cut out their rabbits. The rabbit eyes also need to be cut.
5. Students hold their rabbit masks and hop "The Bunny Hop," which may be found online. The music teacher may want to help with "The Bunny Hop"!

Learning Styles

Linguistic (hearing stories), spatial (coloring), bodily kinesthetic (acting), musical (dancing), and intrapersonal (working alone).

Teaching Team

Music, library, and science teachers.

Suggested Sources

DePaola, Tomie. *Too Many Bunnies*. Mahwah, NJ: Troll, 1989.[Fiction]
Doudna, Kelly. *Bunnies*. Minneapolis, MN: Abdo, 1999. [Nonfiction]
Gibbons, Gail. *Rabbits, Rabbits, and More Rabbits*. New York: Holiday House, 2000. [Nonfiction]
Tafuri, Nancy. *Will You Be My Friend?* New York: Scholastic, 2001. [Fiction]
Wells, Rosemary. *Bunny Cakes*. New York: Puffin, 2000. [Fiction}
World Book. *World Book Encyclopedia*. Chicago, IL: World Book, 2004.
The following site is the lyrics to the Bunny Hop:
http://www.niehs.nih.gov/kids/lyrics/bunnyhop.htm

Alligator Trouble

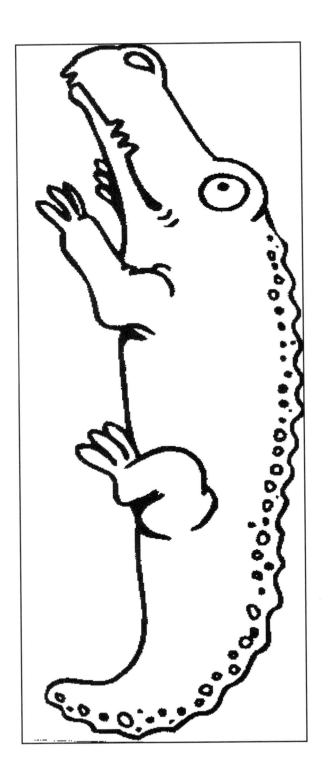

Alligator Trouble

Standards

Students will

- Know the elements that compose a story (e.g., character, plot, events, setting). (McREL 8)
- Know the difference between fact and fiction, real and make believe. (McREL 9)
- Appreciate and enjoy literature and other creative expressions. (AASL/AECT 5)

Objectives

Students hear and discuss fiction books featuring alligators. They discuss plot, character, and setting. Students color and cut out alligators for windsocks or bookmarks.

Directions

1. Gallon-size clear plastic bags are needed if windsocks will be made.
2. The library and reading teachers read two fiction alligator books.
3. Plot, character, setting, and the reasons why they are fiction are discussed.
4. Students color and cut out their alligators.
5. Students may make bicycle windsocks with the help of the art teacher. Student alligators are glued onto clear gallon-size plastic bags. Five to six twelve-inch ribbon streamers or colorful paper strips are added along the bag bottom. A handle measuring twelve-inches long and three inches wide, made of ribbon or a paper strip, is attached at the top of one bag layer, leaving the bag open for wind breezes.
6. Instead of making a windsock, students may simply use their alligators for bookmarks.

Learning Styles

Linguistic (hearing books, discussing), spatial (coloring), interpersonal (discussing), and intrapersonal (making a windsock or bookmark).

Teaching Team

Art, library, and reading teachers.

Suggested Sources

Cole, Joanna. *Gator Girls*. New York: Morrow, 1995.
Hurd, Thatcher. *Mama Don't Allow*. New York: HarperTrophy, 1985.
Mayer, Mercer. *There's an Alligator Under My Bed*. New York: Dial, 2005.
Mozelle, Shirley. *Zack's Alligator*. New York: HarperTrophy, 1995.

Chapter 3

Second Grade Lesson Plans

A solid, professionally based library lesson plan is built around developmental needs of students at their grade level, around the McREL or Kendall and Marzano National Education Language Arts Standards and Benchmarks, the AASL (American Association of School Libraries), and the AECT (Association for Educational Communications and Technology) Information Literacy Standards, and around the various learning styles of students as found in Gardner's Multiple Intelligences framework. (The selected AASL/AECT standards and Gardner's Multiple Intelligences are fully described in the introduction.) All of the following lessons are built around these standards, benchmarks, and skills in order to ensure that all students appreciate different forms of literature and are competent users of information, and so become information literate.

Each lesson plan includes student objectives, team teaching suggestions, and suggested sources. Furthermore, each lesson is designed to last approximately twenty minutes. All lessons have been field-tested. The lessons provide individual or small-group worksheet work and are designed to make library learning enjoyable, to be easily accomplished in a librarian's or library teacher's busy schedule, and to be grounded in rigorous standards and benchmarks. Each lesson has a direct reference to the following McREL standards and benchmarks, as well as a direct reference to the AASL/AECT standards.

Second Grade Library Standards and Language Arts Benchmarks (McREL)

Reprinted by permission of McREL

Second grade students will be able to:

Use the general skills and strategies of the writing process. (Standard 1)

1. Use writing and other methods (e.g., using letters) to describe. (Standard 1, Benchmark 6)

Gather and use information for research purposes. (Standard 4)

2. Use a variety of sources to gather information (e.g., informational books, pictures, charts, indexes, videos, Internet). (Standard 4, Benchmark 2)
3. Use encyclopedias to gather information. (Standard 4, Benchmark 2, under grades 3–5)
4. Use maps to get information. (Standard 4, Benchmark 6, under grades 3–5)

Use the general skills and strategies of the reading process. (Standard 5)

5. Know that books have titles, authors, and often illustrators. (Standard 5, Benchmark 12)

Use reading skills and strategies to understand and interpret a variety of literary texts. (Standard 6)

6. Use reading skills and strategies to understand a variety of familiar literary text (e.g., fairy tales, folktales, fiction, nonfiction, legends, fables, myths, poems, nursery rhymes, picture books, predictable books). (Standard 6, Benchmark 1)
7. Know the elements that compose a story (e.g., character, plot, events, setting). (Standard 6, Benchmark 2, under Pre-K)
8. Know the difference between fact and fiction, real and make-believe. (Standard 6, Benchmark 4, under Pre-K)

Use reading skills and strategies to understand and interpret a variety of informational texts. (Standard 7)

9. Use the various parts of a book. (Standard 7, Benchmark 4, under grades 3–5)
10. Use prior knowledge and experience to understand and respond to new information. (Standard 7, Benchmark 6, under grades 3–5)

Use listening and speaking strategies for different purposes. (Standard 8)

11. Create or act out familiar stories, rhymes, and plays. (Standard 8, Benchmark 9, under Pre-K)

Using a Compass Rose

Using a Compass Rose

Look at the compass and the map! Where are things at school?

1. Where is the slide from the school?   North South West East

2. Where is the bus from the school?   North South West East

3. Where is the tree from the school?   North South West East

4. Where are the swings from school?   North South West East

Using a Compass Rose

Standards

Students will

- Use maps to get information. (McREL 4)
- Access information efficiently and effectively. (AASL/AECT 1)
- Strive for excellence in information seeking and knowledge generation. (AASL/AECT 6)

Objectives

Students use a compass rose to answer the questions about their worksheet maps. Students color their worksheets.

Directions

1. The library teacher creates an overhead transparency or a computerized scan of the student worksheet copy.
2. The social studies teacher reviews cardinal directions with the students, having them stand facing north, secondly turn to face south, thirdly point a thumb to the west, and then finally wave toward the east.
3. The library and social studies teachers show and describe the compass rose picture on the worksheet.
4. In response to each question, students circle a direction on their sheets after looking at the map and compass rose. Teachers check for understanding.
5. Students color their sheets.
6. If time permits, students may browse any available atlases to become more familiar with atlases.

Learning Styles

Mathematical (thinking logically), spatial (coloring, reading maps), intrapersonal (working alone).

Teaching Team

Library and social studies teachers.

Suggested Sources

Any available atlases.

Tigers

The shirt, the coat, and the shoes.

Tigers, you loose!

Write a rhyming poem of 2 or 3 lines about the story at the bottom of the page

_____

_____

Tigers

Standards

Students will

- Use writing and other methods to describe. (McREL 1)
- Use reading skills and strategies to understand a variety of familiar literary passages and f text (e.g., fairy tales, folktales, fiction, nonfiction, legends, fables, myths, poems, nursery rhymes, picture books, predictable books). (McREL 6)
- Know the elements that compose a story (e.g., character, plot, events, setting). (McREL 7)
- Appreciate and enjoy literature and other creative expressions of information. (AASL/AECT 5)
- Recognize the importance of information to a democratic society. (AASL/AECT 7)
- Participate effectively in groups to pursue and generate information. (AASL/AECT 9)

Objectives

Students hear and see a version of *Little Black Sambo*. The class explains the setting, main plot, and main character, and composes a two- or three-line poem about it.

Directions

1. The library teacher reads or tells a version of *Little Black Sambo*, like *The Story of Little Babaji* or *Sam and the Tigers*. While reading it, illustrations are shown.
2. Then the class discusses plot, setting, and main character.
3. The reading teacher has the class compose a two- or three-line poem about the story. The teacher reads a couple of short poems to give students ideas. Students may also write the poem given in the worksheet directions.
4. After writing the poem, students color their sheets.

Learning Styles

Linguistic (hearing stories, writing), spatial (coloring), musical (poetry rhythm), interpersonal (class discussion and class poetry), and intrapersonal (working alone).

Teaching Team

Library and reading teachers.

Suggested Sources

Bannerman, Helen. *The Story of Little Babaji*. New York: HarperCollins, 1996.
Calmenson, Stephanie and Joanna Cole. *Read, Set, Read!* New York: Doubleday, 1990. [poems]
Pinkney, Jerry. *Sam and the Tigers*. New York: Dial, 1996.
Prelutsky, Jack. *For Laughing Out Loud*. New York: Alfred A. Knopf, 1991. [poems]

Tornado!

Find two facts about tornadoes. Write the facts in the clouds.
Then color the picture.

Tornado!

Standards

Students will

- Use writing and other methods (e.g., using letters) to describe. (McREL 1)
- Use a variety of sources to gather information (e.g., informational books, pictures, charts, indexes, videos, Internet). (McREL 2)
- Use encyclopedias to gather information. (McREL 3)
- Use prior knowledge and experience to understand and respond to new information. (McREL 10)
- Access information efficiently and effectively. (AASL/AECT 1)
- Evaluate information critically and competently. (AASL/AECT 2)
- Use information effectively and creatively. (AASL/AECT 3)
- Recognize the importance of information to a democratic society. (AASL/AECT 7)
- Participate effectively in groups to pursue and generate information. (AASL/AECT 9)

Objectives

Student groups read, view, and share tornado facts. Students write two facts and then color their sheets.

Directions

1. The teachers asks students what they already know about tornadoes.
2. Small student groups use nonfiction books on tornadoes and/or encyclopedias to locate some tornado facts and pictures.
3. Teachers list four to five simple tornado facts on the board from students' research.
4. Students copy two facts from the board on their tornado sheets, then color their sheets.
5. If time permits, students may locate and add more facts on their sheets.

Learning Styles

Linguistic (reading, writing), mathematical (thinking logically), spatial (coloring), interpersonal (collecting facts), and intrapersonal (writing facts).

Teaching Team

Library and social studies teachers.

Suggested Sources

Burby, Liza N. *Tornadoes*. New York: PowerKids, 1999.
Galiano, Dean. *Tornadoes*. New York: Rosen Publishing, 2000.
Nicolson, Cynthia Pratt. *Tornado!* Minneapolis, MN: Sagebrush Ed., 2003.
World Book Encyclopedia. Chicago, IL: World Book, 2004.

Cats, Cats, Cats

This cat has a front and a back side.

What color will you make both sides of it?

Put a face on the front.

Cut out both cat squares together.

Fold on the dotted line to make a cute kitty desk decoration.

Cats, Cats, Cats

Standards

Students will

- Use writing and other methods to describe. (McREL 1)
- Use reading skills and strategies to understand and interpret a variety of familiar literary texts (e.g., fairy tales, folktales, fiction, nonfiction, legends, fables, myths, poems, nursery rhymes, picture books, predictable books). (McREL 6)
- Know the elements that compose a story (e.g., character, plot, events, setting). (McREL 7)
- Know the difference between fact and fiction, real and make-believe. (McREL 8)
- Appreciate and enjoy literature and other creative expression (AASL/AECT 5)
- Participate effectively in groups to pursue and generate information. (AASL/AECT 9)

Objectives

Students hear two fiction books about cats. They discuss the plot, character, setting, and the reason why the books are fiction. Students write a short word script, then color and create a cat desk decoration.

Directions

1. The reading or library teacher reads and shows two fiction books about cats. Teachers may read cat books in the fall or at Halloween.
2. Students discuss plot, character, setting, and why the books are fiction.
3. The class brainstorms words for their cat to say, as inspired from the books heard. Teachers write the cat sayings or scripts on the board.
4. Students write a cat script in the cat callout on their worksheets.
5. Students color both of the cats the identical color, and add facial parts, such as eyes, to the cat on one side. The cats may be colored black for fall or Halloween.
6. Students cut around the two cat squares, and then fold in the middle.
7. The cats are a freestanding desk decoration.

Learning Styles

Linguistic (writing), spatial (coloring), and interpersonal (discussing).

Teaching Team

Language arts and library teachers.

Suggested Sources

Bonsall, Crosby. *The Case of the Cat's Meow*. New York: HarperCollins, 1978.
Bunting, Eve. *Scary, Scary Halloween*. New York: Clarion, 1986.
Henkes, Kevin. *Kitten's First Full Moon*. New York: HarperCollins, 2004.
McCarty, Peter. *Hondo and Fabian*. New York: Scholastic, 2003.
Myers, Christopher. *Black Cat*. New York: Scholastic, 1999.

Find the Number

Encyclopedias have information on almost everything! The books of an encyclopedia are called **volumes**.

Find the following words in the encyclopedia.

Write the encyclopedia volume number. Write the page number.

Mars

Volume: Page:

Duck

Volume: Page:

Python

Volume: Page:

Lincoln

Volume: Page:

Statue of Liberty

Volume: Page:

Banana

Volume: Page:

Find the Number

Standards

Students will

- Use writing and other methods (e.g., using letters) to describe. (McREL 1)
- Use encyclopedias to gather information. (McREL 3)
- Use prior knowledge and experience to understand and respond to new information. (McREL 10)
- Access information efficiently and effectively. (AASL/AECT 1)
- Use information effectively and creatively. (AASL/AECT 3)
- Strive for excellence in information seeking and knowledge generation. (AASL/AECT 6)
- Participate effectively in groups to pursue and generate information. (AASL/AECT 9)

Objectives

Students learn how to use encyclopedias to find information, and become familiar with the term *volume*. Students write the volume and page numbers for subjects on their worksheet.

Directions

1. The library teacher explains how encyclopedias have facts on almost anything in separate "books" called *volumes*. The teacher shows how to find information in the encyclopedia by using guidewords.
2. The library teacher shows students how to locate the first worksheet subject in the encyclopedia, and then writes down the volume and page number on the board so that the entire class has full understanding of the worksheet.
3. The language arts and library teachers guide student pairs as they find the rest of the worksheet subjects.
4. Once students are checked for excellence in learning by successfully locating all of the subjects, they may color the worksheets.
5. In any remaining time, students may simply browse encyclopedias.

Learning Styles

Linguistic (reading, writing), spatial (coloring), mathematical (thinking logically), and interpersonal (working in groups).

Teaching Team

Language arts and library teachers.

Suggested Sources

World Book. *World Book Encyclopedia.* Chicago, IL: World Book, 2004.

Who's Out Tonight?

Some animals go out in the night. They are called *nocturnal* animals. Who are they? Color the night sky dark. Color and cut out a nocturnal animal. Glue it in the picture. In the long box, write about it.

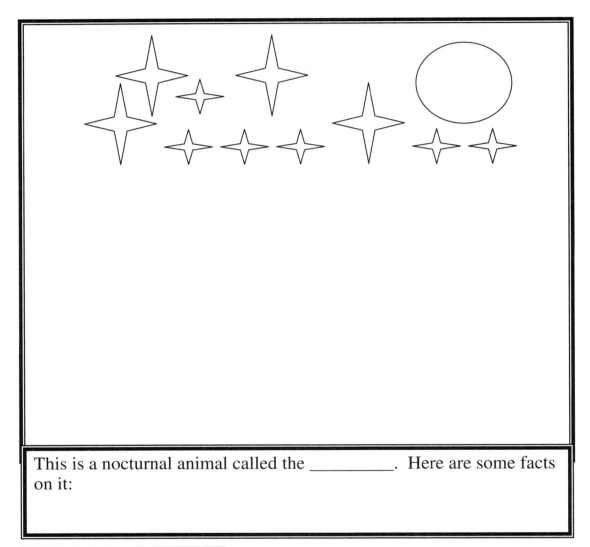

This is a nocturnal animal called the _____. Here are some facts on it:

Who's Out Tonight?

Standards

Students will

- Use writing and other methods (e.g., using letters) to describe. (McREL 1)
- Use a variety of sources to gather information (e.g., informational books, pictures, charts, indexes, videos, Internet). (McREL 2)
- Use encyclopedias to gather information. (McREL 3)
- Access information efficiently and effectively. (AASL/AECT 1)
- Evaluate information critically and competently. (AASL/AECT 2)
- Use information effectively and creatively. (AASL/AECT 3)
- Strive for excellence in information seeking and knowledge generation. (AASL/AECT 6)

Objectives

Students color a night scene and three nocturnal animals (skunk, fox, bat). They glue one or more animals on the night scene. They research and write facts.

Directions

1. The science teacher discusses the term *nocturnal* and lists some nocturnal animals on the board.
2. The library teacher pulls nonfiction books about skunks, foxes, and bats.
3. Students color the skunk, fox, and bat the correct colors after finding pictures.
4. Students choose one animal and writes one or more facts on their sheets.
5. After the worksheet night scene is colored, students cut out one or more of the nocturnal animals and glue them into the scene.
6. If time permits, teachers may help students locate and write more facts for the other animals on a separate sheet of blank paper to be stapled to the back of the worksheet. More fact collecting may also be completed during science class.

Learning Styles

Linguistic (read, write), spatial (coloring), interpersonal (group work), and intrapersonal (working alone).

Teaching Team

Library and science teachers.

Suggested Sources

Behm, Barbara. *Daytime and Nighttime Animals.* Milwaukee, WI: Gareth Stevens, 1999.
Heinrichs, Ann. *Bats.* Minneapolis, MN: Compass Point Books, 2004.
Lepthien, Emilie U. *Skunks.* Chicago, IL: Children's Press, 1993.
Olien, Becky. *Foxes: Clever Hunters.* Mankato, MN: Capstone, 2002.
World Book Encyclopedia. Chicago, IL: World Book, 2004.

Giving Thanks

Give thanks by making and giving Thanksgiving napkin holders.

Giving Thanks

Standards

Students will

- Know that books have titles, authors, and often illustrators. (McREL 5)
- Use reading skills and strategies to understand a variety of familiar literary text (e.g., fairy tales, folktales, fiction, nonfiction, legends, fables, myths, poems, nursery rhymes, picture books, predictable books). (McREL 6)
- Use prior knowledge and experience to understand and respond to new information. (McREL 10)
- Use information effectively and creatively. (AASL/AECT 3)
- Recognize the importance of information to a democratic society. (AASL/AECT 7)

Objectives

Students listen to and discuss two books on how Thanksgiving is celebrated today. They review title, author, and illustrator. They make Thanksgiving napkin holders.

Directions

1. Duplicate three more strips like the blank strip on the worksheet.
2. The social studies or library teacher reads two Thanksgiving fiction stories that demonstrate how Thanksgiving is celebrated. Title, author, and illustrator are pointed out.
3. After the books are read, students explain how Thanksgiving is celebrated, and then compare the stories to how they personally celebrate Thanksgiving.
4. Students make Thanksgiving napkin holders. They color and cut out the Thanksgiving worksheet squares.
5. The duplicated worksheet strips are also colored and cut out. Each strip will be taped at the ends to form a large circle.
6. Each worksheet square is attached on the top of one of the circled strips. Teachers demonstrate how the resulting napkin holder works.
7. Students may give away their napkin holders to their family or to others.

Learning Styles

Spatial (coloring, creating) and intrapersonal (working alone).

Teaching Team

Library and social studies teachers.

Suggested Sources

Goode, Diane. *Thanksgiving Is Here!* New York: HarperCollins, 2002.
Kendall, Russ. *Giving Thanks.* New York: Scholastic, 2001.
Livingston, Myra Cohn. *Thanksgiving Poems.* New York: Holiday House, 1985.
Spinelli, Eileen. *Thanksgiving at Tappleton's.* New York: HarperCollins, 1992.
Watson, Wendy. *Thanksgiving at Our House.* New York: Clarion, 1991.

The Bull

What did the bull like to do? _____

Draw what changed the bulls' mind.

How did the story end? _____

_____

The Bull

Standards

Students will

- Use writing and other methods to describe. (McREL 1)
- Know that books have titles, authors, and often illustrators. (McREL 5)
- Know the elements that compose a story (e.g., character, plot, events, setting). (McREL 7)
- Appreciate and enjoy literature and other creative expressions of information. (AASL/AECT 5)
- Participate effectively in groups to pursue and generate information. (AASL/AECT 9)

Objectives

Students listen to a fictional story about a bull. They discuss title, author, and illustrator. Students recall beginning, middle, and ending plots, and the main character. Students answer and color their worksheets.

Directions

1. The reading and library teachers read a fiction book about a bull. The title, author, and illustrator are discussed.
2. The beginning, main, and ending plots are discussed, along with the main character.
3. The class first answers the worksheet questions orally, as the teachers prompt for and write the answers on the board.
4. Then students copy the answers from the board on their worksheets. They also draw what changed the bull's mind on their worksheets.
5. Finally, students the scene on their worksheets.

Learning Styles

Linguistic (writing), spatial (coloring), interpersonal (answering questions), and intrapersonal (drawing).

Teaching Team

Library and reading teachers.

Suggested Sources

Leaf, Munro. *The Story of Ferdinand.* New York: Grosset & Dunlap, 2000.
Schnetzler, Pattie. *Widdermaker.* Minneapolis, MN: Carolrhoda, 2002.

Puppet

Put Pinocchio together!

From Joyce Keeling, *Lesson Plans for the Busy Librarian: A Standards Based Approach for the Elementary Library Media Center*, Volume 2. Westport, CT: Libraries Unlimited. © 2006.

Puppet

Standards

Students will

- Use reading skills and strategies to understand a variety of familiar literary texts (e.g., fairy tales, folktales, fiction, nonfiction, legends, fables, myths, poems, nursery rhymes, picture books, predictable books). (McREL 6)
- Know the elements that compose a story (e.g., character, plot, events, setting). (McREL 7)
- Create or act out familiar stories, rhymes, and plays. (McREL 11)
- Appreciate and enjoy literature and other creative expressions of information. (AASL/AECT 5)
- Participate effectively in groups to pursue and generate information. (AASL/AECT 9)

Objectives

Students listen to *Pinocchio* and discover why it's a fairy tale. They discuss the main plot, characters, events, and setting. They create a puppet to show the story.

Directions

1. The reading and library teachers read or tell a simple *Pinocchio* story. While telling the story, teachers point out why the story is a fairy tale.
2. Students discuss plot, characters, events, and setting.
3. Students color their worksheet puppet.
4. The art teacher helps students put their puppets together. The puppet arms and legs are attached with short brad fasteners.
5. A heavy string or ribbon is attached to the top of the puppet.
6. In small groups, students act out the *Pinocchio* plot with their puppets.

Learning Styles

Linguistic (telling the story plot), spatial (creating a puppet), bodily kinesthetic (acting), and interpersonal (working with others).

Teaching Team

Art, library, and reading teachers.

Suggested Sources

Assensio, Agusti. *Pinocchio*. Spain: The Child's World, 1988.

Bell, Edward. *Pinocchio*. New York: HBO Kids, 1997. [Videorecording]

Weber, Louis. "Pinoccchio." In *Treasury of Fairy Tales*. Lincolnwood, IL: Publications International, 1997.

Winkleman, Barbara Games. *Pinocchio's Nose Grows*. New York: Random House, 2002.

Find a Book

1st—Find a book on the shelf. Write down the author, title, and call number.

2nd—Now use the Card Catalog. Find the book in the Card Catalog.

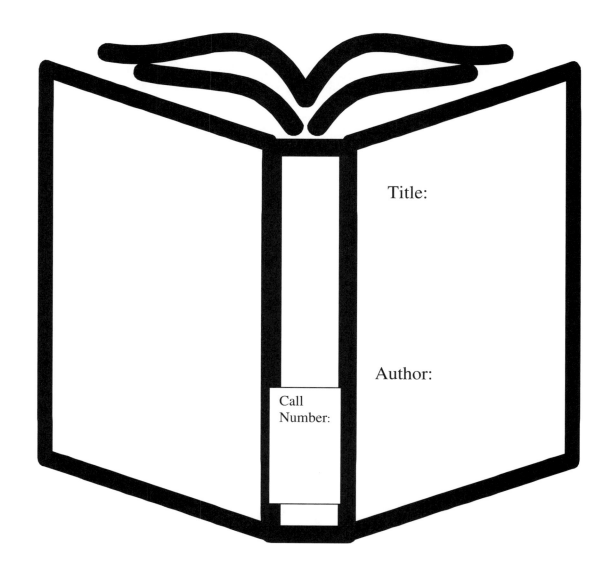

Title:

Author:

Call Number:

Find a Book

Standards

Students will

- Use writing and other methods (e.g., using letters) to describe. (McREL 1)
- Know that books have titles, authors, and often illustrators. (McREL 5)
- Use prior knowledge and experience to understand and respond to new information. (McREL 10)
- Access information efficiently and effectively. (AASL/AECT 1)
- Practice ethical behavior in regard to information and information technology. (AASL/ AAECT 8)

Objectives

Students find the title, author, and call number of a book and write those facts on their worksheets. Students learn how to find their book on the card catalog.

Directions

1. Make an overhead transparency of the student worksheet.
2. Using four or five selected books, the library teacher demonstrates how to find the title, author, and call number of a book, writing the information on the transparency.
3. Students then choose a book from the library shelves and fill in the book title, author, and call number on their worksheets.
4. Teachers check student worksheets for accuracy.
5. Students find their books on the card catalog with the teachers' help.

Learning Styles

Linguistic (reading and writing), bodily kinesthetic (finding book, using card catalog), and intrapersonal (working alone).

Teaching Team

Library and reading teachers.

Suggested Sources

Library and Card Catalog

Twelve Days of Christmas

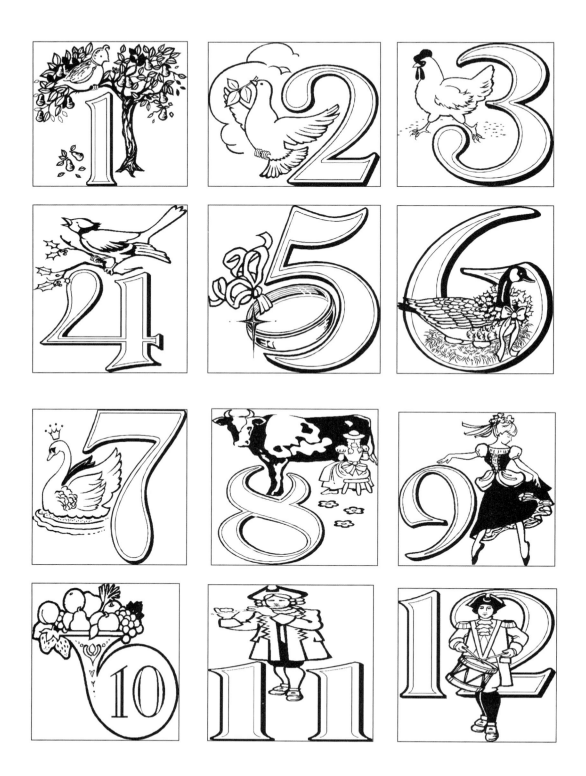

From Joyce Keeling, *Lesson Plans for the Busy Librarian: A Standards Based Approach for the Elementary Library Media Center*, Volume 2. Westport, CT: Libraries Unlimited. © 2006.

Twelve Days of Christmas

Standards

Students will

- Use writing and other methods to describe. (McREL 1)
- Use reading skills and strategies to understand a variety of familiar literary text(e.g., fairy tales, folktales, fiction, nonfiction, legends, fables, myths, poems, nursery rhymes, picture books, predictable books). (McREL 6)
- Know the elements that compose a story (e.g., characters, setting, events). (McREL 7)
- Appreciate and enjoy literature and other creative expressions of information. (AASL/AECT 5)

Objectives

Students listen to the *The Twelve Days of Christmas* as it is read to them. They review the story events and make a Christmas wreath using the twelve event days from the story. Students sing *The Twelve Days of Christmas.*

Directions

1. Students listen to *The Twelve Days of Christmas* as it is read to them.
2. The library teacher prompts students to recall the order of events by reviewing the book illustrations.
3. Students color the squares on their worksheets.
4. The art teacher helps students make a wreath of the twelve days of Christmas. The wreath size is the size of a larger dinner plate. The wreath may be made out of a circle of heavy-weight paper or an actual large paper dinner plate, and colored green.
5. Students cut out their twelve colored squares and glue them on the paper wreath.
6. The music teacher may lead the students in singing *The Twelve Days of Christmas.*

Learning Styles

Spatial (creating), bodily kinesthetic (doing crafts), musical (singing), and intrapersonal (working alone).

Teaching Team

Art, library, and music teachers.

Suggested Sources

Brett, Jan. *The Twelve Days of Christmas.* New York: G.P. Putnam's Sons, 1989.
Daily, Don. *Twelve Days of Christmas.* Philadelphia, PA: Running Press Books, 2000.
Knight, Hilary. *The Twelve Days of Christmas.* New York: Macmillan, 1983.
Wonder Kids Choir. *100 Christmas Songs for Kids.* New York: Time-Life Warner, 2004. [CD]

The Dragon

Make a dragon. Color the dragon's head and strip. Fold the strip many times. Connect the strip to the dragon's head to make the dragon's body.

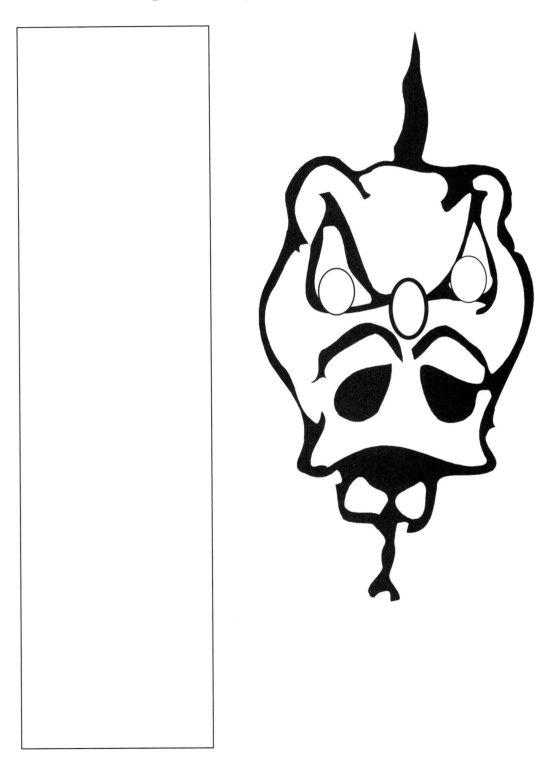

The Dragon

Standards

Students will

- Use reading skills and strategies to understand a variety of familiar literary text (e.g., fairy tales, folktales, fiction, nonfiction, legends, fables, myths, poems, nursery rhymes, picture books, predictable books). (McREL 6)
- Know the elements that compose a story (e.g., character, plot, events, setting). (McREL 7)
- Create or act out familiar stories, rhymes, and plays. (McREL 11)
- Recognize the importance of information to a democratic society. (AASL/AECT 7)
- Participate effectively in groups to pursue and generate information. (AASL/AECT 9)

Objectives

Students learn about Chinese New Year. They make Chinese dragons, and act out a Chinese dragon story. They discuss plot, character, and setting.

Directions

1. The library teacher introduces the lesson by briefly stating a few Chinese New Year facts and the connection with dragons. The teacher reads and shows a fictional Chinese dragon book.
2. After hearing the dragon story, students discuss main character, plot, and setting.
3. The art teacher helps students create dragons. Students color the dragon's head and body strip. The body strip is folded accordion-style and joined to the dragon's head.
4. In front of small groups, students act out the dragon story with their dragons.

Learning Styles

Linguistic (hearing a story), spatial (creating), bodily kinesthetic (acting), interpersonal (discussing), and intrapersonal (acting out the story).

Teaching Team

Art and library teachers.

Suggested Sources

Flanagan, Alice K. *Chinese New Year*. Minneapolis, MN: Compass, 2004. [nonfiction]
Nunes, Susan Miho. *The Last Dragon*. New York: Scholastic, 1990. [fiction]
Schaefer, Lola. M. *Chinese New Year*. Mankato, MN: Pebble Books, 2001. [nonfiction]
Waters, Kate and Madeline Slovenz-Low. *Lion Dancer*. New York: Scholastic, 1995. [fiction]
World Book. *Childcraft: The How and Why Library*. Chicago, IL: World Book, 2004.

Forming Dinosaur Facts

Find facts on dinosaurs from nonfiction books.
Write the facts around the dinosaur!

Forming Dinosaur Facts

Standards

Students will

- Use writing and other methods (e.g., using letters) to describe. (McREL 1)
- Use a variety of sources to gather information (e.g., informational books, pictures, charts, indexes, videos, Internet). (McREL 2)
- Know the difference between fact and fiction, real and make-believe. (McREL 8)
- Access information efficiently and effectively. (AASL/AECT 1)
- Evaluate information critically and competently. (AASL/AECT 2)
- Use information effectively and creatively. (AASL/AECT 3)
- Pursue information related to personal interests. (AASL/AECT 4)
- Practice ethical behavior in regard to information and information technology. (AASL/AECT 8)

Objectives

Students define nonfiction. Students find dinosaur facts and write a shape poem around their worksheet dinosaurs.

Directions

1. The library teacher displays several nonfiction books about dinosaurs. and shows why they are nonfiction. The call number is also explained.
2. Library and science teachers help students find dinosaur facts from nonfiction books. Students write their facts around the worksheet dinosaurs, to create shape poems.
3. Teachers monitor students and remind them not to copy word by word.
4. Students color their dinosaurs.

Learning Styles

Mathematical (thinking logically), linguistic (writing), spatial (coloring), interpersonal (working in groups), and intrapersonal (working alone).

Teaching Team

Library and science teachers.

Suggested Sources

Amery, Heather. *Looking at ... Brachiosaurus.* Milwaukee, WI: Gareth Stevens, 1993.
Cohen, Daniel. *Allosaurus.* Mankato, MN: Bridgestone Press, 2003.
Landau, Elaine. *Apatosaurus.* New York: Children's Press, 1999.
Wilkes, Angela. *The Big Book of Dinosaurs.* New York: Dorling Kindersley, 1994.
Zallinger, Peter. *Dinosaurs.* New York: Random House, 1977.
Zoehfeld, Kathleen. *Dinosaurs Big and Small.* New York: HarperCollins, 2002.

Clowning Around

Book Cover

How to be a Clown!

By Theresa Rod

Table of Contents for the book

Table of Contents

Chapter	Page
Jokes	4
Cloths	7
Makeup	10
Tricks	13
Circus Jobs	15

1. What is the title for the clown book? _____

_____

2. Who is the author? _____

3. Look at the Table of Contents. It tells the chapters and pages of the clown book.
   Where is the chapter on tricks?   Page_____
   Where is the chapter on jokes?   Page_____

4. What would you like to learn about clowns?_____

_____

From Joyce Keeling, *Lesson Plans for the Busy Librarian: A Standards Based Approach for the Elementary Library Media Center*, Volume 2. Westport, CT: Libraries Unlimited. © 2006.

Clowning Around

Standards

Students will

- Use writing and other methods (e.g., using letters) to describe. (McREL 1)
- Use reading skills and strategies to understand a variety of familiar literary passages (e.g., fairy tales, folktales, fiction, nonfiction, legends, fables, myths, poems, nursery rhymes, picture books, predictable books). (McREL 6)
- Use the various parts of a book. (McREL 9)
- Strive for excellence in information seeking and knowledge generation. (AASL/AECT 6)
- Recognize the importance of information to a democratic society (AASL/AECT 7)

Objectives

Students discuss what is on a book cover, and learn how to use a table of contents. They answer questions about the book cover and table of contents using the worksheet example.

Directions

1. The library teacher discusses what is on a book cover by showing several books examples.
2. The language arts teacher discusses the table of contents and gives examples from several books.
3. Students look at the example of a book cover and table of contents on their worksheet, and answer the questions.
4. In any remaining time, students may use the table of contents from various simple books and share simple facts from them. Teachers monitor students for understanding.

Learning Styles

Linguistic (reading, writing) and intrapersonal (working alone).

Teaching Team

Language arts and library teachers.

Suggested Sources

Simple books that have tables of contents.

Valentine's Day Hearts

Valentine's Day Hearts

Standards

Students will

- Use writing and other methods to describe. (McREL 1)
- Use a variety of resources to gather information (e.g., informational books, pictures, charts, indexes, videos, Internet). (McREL 2)
- Use prior knowledge and experience to understand and respond to new information. (McREL 10)
- Appreciate and enjoy literature and other creative expressions of information. (AASL/AECT 5)

Objectives

Students listen to a fictional Valentine's book. They brainstorm adjectives that reflect Valentine's Day. They write a Valentine's adjective on each small heart on the worksheet and glue the hearts on a sack.

Directions

1. Brown or white paper sacks are needed for this activity.
2. Copy student worksheet on pink or pastel-colored sheets of paper.
3. The language arts teacher reads a fun book on adjectives.
4. The library teacher reads a Valentine's fictional book that mentions hearts.
5. On the board, teachers write adjectives, suggested by the class, that are used on Valentine's Day. Such words may be cute, sweet, nice, and others as found in the books.
6. Students write Valentine's adjectives on as many worksheet hearts as possible.
7. Students cut out and glue the hearts on small brown or white sacks. The sacks may either hold student Valentine's cards or be used as a gift. The hearts may also be glued on a folded sheet of blank paper for a Valentine's card.

Learning Styles

Linguistic (writing), spatial (creating), interpersonal (group work), and intrapersonal (working alone).

Teaching Team

Language arts and library teachers.

Suggested Sources

Brown, Marc. *Arthur's Valentine*. Boston, MA: Little, Brown and Company, 1988.

Cleary, Brian P. *Hairy, Scary, Ordinary: What is an Adjective?* Minneapolis, MN: Carolrhoda, 2000.

Heller, Ruth. *Many Luscious Lollipops: A Book about Adjectives*. New York: Putnam & Grosset, 1989.

Lexauri, Joan M. *Don't Be My Valentine*. New York: Harper & Row, 1999.

Snake Is Loose!

The snake is loose! Oh, my!

Color it. Cut it out.

Keep it safe by wrapping around your pencil!

Snake Is Loose!

Standards

Students will

- Use reading skills and strategies to understand a variety of familiar literary passages and familiar literary texts (e.g., fairy tales, folktales, fiction, nonfiction, legends, fables, myths, poems, nursery rhymes, picture books, predictable books). (McREL 6)
- Know the elements that compose a story (character, plot, events, setting). (McREL 7)
- Appreciate and enjoy literature and other creative expressions of information. (AASL/AECT 5)

Objectives

Students listen to two fiction books about snakes. They discuss plot, main character, and setting. Students color, cut out, and create pencil wraps.

Directions

1. The library teacher reads two fiction books about snakes.
2. Plot, main character, and setting are discussed.
3. Students color their worksheet snakes.
4. The art teacher instructs students on how to make snake pencil wraps. Students cut out the snake box. They may need help cutting the pencil slits (unless an adult volunteer has cut the slits already).
5. Thread pencils in and out of the snake slits to make it look like the snake is wrapping itself around a pencil.
6. If time permits, students may listen to or create snake jokes.

Learning Style

Spatial (coloring, creating), interpersonal (discussing), and intrapersonal (working alone).

Teaching Team

The art and library teachers.

Suggested Sources

Buckley, Richard. *The Greedy Python.* Natick, MA: Picture Book Studies, 1985.
Cannon, Janelle. *Verdi.* New York: HarperCollins, 1995.
Coxe, Molly. *The Great Snake Escape.* New York: HarperCollins, 1994.
Namm, Diane. *Slithery, Squirmy Jokes.* New York: Barnes & Noble, 2001. [jokes]
Noble, Trinka H. *Jimmy's Boa and the Big Birthday Bash.* New York: HarperCollins, 1995.
Provenchen, Rose-Marie. *Slithery Jake.* New York: HarperCollins, 2004.

Saint Patrick's Day

What is Saint Patrick's Day?

1. Saint Patrick's Day is to celebrate Color Ireland.

2. Circle two things that tell about Saint Patrick's Day.

   Parades   Turkeys   Green Clothes

3. Circle why green is worn for Saint Patrick's Day.

   Green is nice.   Green is the color of Ireland.

4. Circle when it is Saint Patrick's Day.

   March 17th   December 25th

5. Color the Shamrock. Cut it out. Wear it!

Saint Patrick's Day

Standards

Students will

- Use writing and other methods (e.g., using letters) to describe. (McREL 1)
- Use a variety of sources to gather information (e.g., informational books, pictures, charts, indexes, videos, Internet). (McREL 2)
- Know that books have titles, authors, and often illustrators. (McREL 5)
- Know the difference between fact and fiction, real and make believe. (McREL 8)
- Evaluate information critically and competently. (AASL/AECT 2)
- Use information effectively and creatively. (AASL/AECT 3)
- Strive for excellence in information seeking and knowledge generation. (AASL/AECT 6)
- Recognize the importance of information to a democratic society. (AASL/AECT 7)

Objectives

Students learn about St. Patrick's Day through fiction and nonfiction sources. They hear and discuss St. Patrick's Day facts. They color and wear shamrocks.

Directions

1. The library teacher reads an easy fiction book about Ireland or St. Patrick's Day, after pointing out the title, author, and call number. Discussion follows.
2. The social studies teacher reads a few St. Patrick's Day facts from a nonfiction source, after pointing out title, author, and call number. Such facts will include the following: there are parades; shamrocks; the wearing of the green, including green hats; the date of St. Patrick's Day; and that people from Ireland traditionally celebrate St. Patrick's Day.
3. Teachers guide students as they answer worksheet questions.
4. Students color and cut out their shamrocks. Shamrocks are attached with double-faced tape to students' shirts.

Learning Styles

Linguistic (writing), spatial (coloring), interpersonal (group work), and intrapersonal (working alone).

Teaching Team

Library and social studies teachers.

Suggested Sources

dePaola, Tommie. *Rourke and the Big Potato*. New York: Penguin, 1992. [fiction]
Gibbons, Gail. *St. Patrick's Day*. New York: Holiday House, 1994.
O'Donnell, Elizabeth Lee. *Patrick's Day*. New York: Morrow Books, 1994. [fiction]
Roop, Peter and Connie Roop. *Let's Celebrate St. Patrick's Day*. New York: Millbrook, 2003.
World Book. *Childcraft: The How and Why Library*. Chicago, IL: World Book, 2004.

Town and Country Mice

The Town Mouse and the Country Mouse lived in different ways. What would they say to each other about where they lived?

Country Mouse:	Town Mouse:
_____	_____
_____	_____
_____	_____

Town and Country Mouse

Standards

Students will

- Use writing and other methods (e.g., using letters) to describe. (McREL 1)
- Use reading skills and strategies to understand a variety of familiar literary text (e.g., fairy tales, folktales, fiction, nonfiction, legends, fables, myths, poems, nursery rhymes, picture books, predictable books). (McREL 6)
- Know the elements that compose a story (e.g., character, plot, events, setting). (McREL 7)
- Use information effectively and creatively. (AASL/AECT 3)
- Appreciate and enjoy literature and other creative expressions of information. (AASL/AECT 5)

Objectives

Students will hear the fable of "The Town Mouse and the Country Mouse," and then explain plot, setting, and main characters. Students will write a quotation from each mouse.

Directions

1. The library teacher reads the fable "The Town Mouse and the Country Mouse." Plot, setting, and main characters are discussed. The library teacher explains why the story is a fable (it has animal characters that talk and has a moral/lesson).
2. The language arts teacher has students think of something that Country Mouse says to Town Mouse. Likewise, students will think of something that Town Mouse says to Country Mouse. Quotations are written on the board.
3. Students write the quotations on the worksheet.
4. Students color their sheets.

Learning Styles

Linguistic (writing), spatial (coloring), and intrapersonal (working alone).

Teaching Team

Library and language arts teachers.

Suggested Sources

Schecter, Ellen. *The Fable of the Town Mouse and the Country Mouse.* New York: Bantam Books, 1995.

Wood, Don and Audrey. *The Little Mouse, The Big Red Strawberry, and the Big Hungry Bear.* Sydney: Child's Play Ltd, 2003.

Stories Have a Surprising Twist!

(1) Color the object a whale's color. (2) Cut it out. (3) Fold it in half from A to B. (4) Shape it by cutting along the dotted lines. (5) Fold the pointed end upward in the shape of a whale's tail. (6) What is it? It could be a whooper of a whale's tale! Add an eye on each side and you will see!

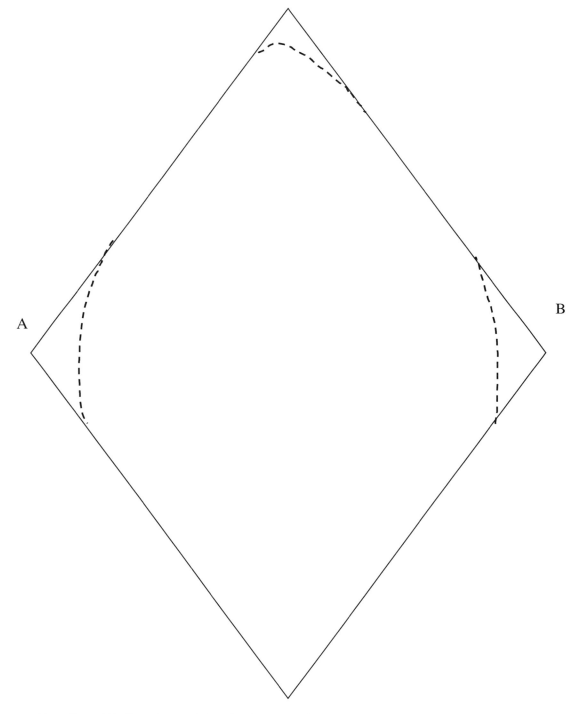

From Joyce Keeling, *Lesson Plans for the Busy Librarian: A Standards Based Approach for the Elementary Library Media Center*, Volume 2. Westport, CT: Libraries Unlimited. © 2006.

Stories Have a Surprising Twist!

Standards

Students will

- Use a variety of sources to gather information (e.g., informational books, pictures, charts, indexes, videos, Internet). (McREL 2)
- Know the elements that compose a story (e.g., character, plot, events, setting). (McREL 7)
- Know the difference between fact and fiction, real and make-believe. (McREL 8)
- Create or act out familiar stories, rhymes, and plays. (McREL 11)
- Evaluate information critically and competently. (AASL/AECT 2)
- Appreciate and enjoy literature and other creative expressions of information. (AASL/AECT 5)
- Participate effectively in groups to pursue and generate information. (AASL/AECT 9)

Objectives

Students hear and discuss a nonfiction and a fiction book about whales. Plot, main character, and story sequence are discussed. Students create a paper-fold whale.

Directions

1. The science teacher shows a book about whales and discusses whale facts, pointing out that the book is nonfiction.
2. The library teacher reads an easy fiction whale book telling that it's fiction.
3. Students discuss plot, main character, and order of events of the fiction book.
4. The art teacher has students color their worksheets, cut out the diamond shape, and fold the shape until a paper whale is made. Students add eyes and other features.
5. Using their whales, students act out the whale story before small class groups.

Learning Styles

Spatial (coloring, creating), bodily kinesthetic (acting), interpersonal (working together), and mathematical (thinking logically).

Teaching Team

Art, library, and science teachers.

Suggested Sources

Drummond, Allan. *Moby Dick*. New York: Farrar, Straus, and Giroux, 1998. [easy book version of the original fiction *Moby Dick*]

Dunbar, Joyce. *Indigo and the Whale*. Mahwah, NJ: Troll, 1996. [fiction]

Holmes, Kevin. *Whales*. Mankato, MN: Capstone, 1998. [nonfiction]

Kristinel, Franklin. *The Gift*. San Francisco: Chronicle Books, 1999. [fiction]

Olien, Becky. *Whales: Giants of the Deep*. Mankato, MN: Capstone, 2002. [nonfiction]

Stars

Stars

Standards

Students will

- Use strategies to understand a variety of familiar literary passages (e.g., fairy tales, folktales, nonfiction, legends, fables, myths, poems, nursery rhymes, picture books, predictable books). (McREL 6)
- Create or act out familiar stories, rhymes, and plays. (McREL 11)
- Evaluate information critically and competently (AASL/AECT 2)
- Appreciate and enjoy literature and other creative expressions of information. (AASL/AECT 5)
- Recognize the importance of information to a democratic society. (AASL/AECT 7)

Objectives

Students hear and then recite facts about stars. Students repeat star poetry. They create star headbands and sing a star song.

Directions

1. Copy the student worksheet onto cardstock paper if desired.
2. The social studies teacher reads and shows a nonfiction book on stars. Students recite a couple of star facts to be written on the board by the teacher.
3. The reading teacher reads one or two short star poems as students repeat them.
4. Students color and cut out the star strips. The stars may be colored patriotically.
5. Staple or tape the strips to fit to each student's head for a star headband.
6. Students sing, "Twinkle, Twinkle, Little Star," led by the music teacher.
7. This activity may be used to celebrate summer, celebrate freedom, or July 4th.

Learning Styles

Musical (repeating poems, singing), spatial (coloring), and intrapersonal (working alone).

Teaching Team

Music, language arts, library, and social studies teachers.

Suggested Sources

Borden, Louise. *America is ...* New York: Margaret McEldeberry Books, 2002. [poetry]
Livingston, Myra Cohn. *Sky Scoop*. New York: Holiday House, 1984. [poetry]
Rustad, Martha E.H. *The Stars*. Minneapolis, MN: Capstone Press, 2002. [nonfiction]
Trapanzi, Iza. *Twinkle, Twinkle, Little Star*. Milwaukee, WI: Gareth Stevens, 1994.
Wandelmaier, Roy. *Stars*. Mahwah, NJ: Troll, 1983. [nonfiction]

Chapter 4

Third Grade Lesson Plans

A solid, professionally based library lesson plan is built around developmental needs of students at their grade level, around the Kendall and Marzano or McREL: National Education Language Arts Standards and Benchmarks, the AASL (American Association of School Libraries), and the AECT (Association for Educational Communications and Technology) Information Literacy Standards, and around the various learning styles of students as found in Gardner's Multiple Intelligences framework. (The selected AASL/AECT standards and Gardner's Multiple Intelligences are fully described in the introduction.) All of the following lessons are built around these standards, benchmarks, and skills in order to ensure that all students appreciate different forms of literature and are competent users of information, and so become information literate.

Each lesson plan includes student objectives, team teaching suggestions, and suggested sources. Furthermore, each lesson is designed to last approximately twenty minutes. All lessons have been field-tested. The lessons provide individual or small-group worksheet work and are designed to make library learning enjoyable, to be easily accomplished in a librarian's or library teacher's busy schedule, and to be grounded in solid standards and benchmarks. Each lesson has a reference to the following McREL standards and benchmarks, as well as a reference to the AASL/AECT standards.

Third Grade Library Standards and Language Arts Benchmarks (McREL)

Reprinted by permission of McREL

Third grade students will be able to:

Use the general skills and strategies of the writing process. (Standard 1)

1. Write in a variety of genres. (Standard 1, Benchmark 7, under grades K–2)

Gather and use information for research purposes. (Standard 4)

2. Use encyclopedias to gather information. (Standard 4, Benchmark 2)
3. Use library catalog. (Standard 4, Benchmark 2, under grades 6–8)
4. Use electronic media to gather information (e.g., Internet, videos). (Standard 4, Benchmark 4)
5. Use key words, guide words, alphabetical and numerical order, indexes, cross references, and letters on volumes to find information for research topics. (Standard 4, Benchmark 5)
6. Use maps to get information. (Standard 4, Benchmark 6)
7. Use a variety of resource materials to gather information for research topics (e.g., magazines, newspapers, dictionaries, schedules, journals, phone directories, globes, atlases, and almanacs). (Standard 4, Benchmark 4, under grades 6–8)

Use reading skills and strategies to understand and interpret a variety of literary texts. (Standard 6)

8. Know the difference between fact and fiction, real and make-believe. (Standard 6, Benchmark 4, under Pre-K)
9. Use reading skills and strategies to understand a variety of familiar literary passages and text (e.g., fairy tales, folktales, fiction, nonfiction, fables, legends, poems, biographies). (Standard 6, Benchmark 1)
10. Know the elements that compose a story (e.g., character, plot, events, setting). (Standard 6, Benchmark 2, under Pre-K)

Use reading skills and strategies to understand and interpret a variety of informational texts. (Standard 7)

11. Use the various parts of a book. (Standard 7, Benchmark 4)

Driving Through Iowa

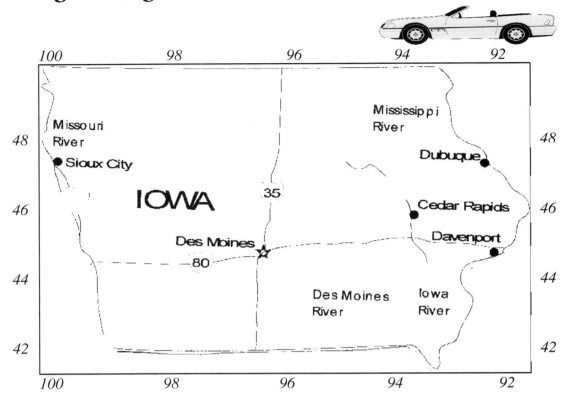

Take a trip through Iowa with this map. This maps has numbers around it to show the degrees of latitude and longitude, called *coordinates*. Coordinates tell you how to get to places. Use this map to answer the following questions.

Before starting your trip, look at the map to learn about the state.

1. What are the four rivers:_____

2. What are the names of the two Interstate roads: _____

Now, start your trip. Write down the map coordinates as you travel.

3. First see Sioux City. What are the coordinates of that city?___, ___

4. Second see Dubuque. What are the coordinates of it?___, ___

5. Finally, visit the state capital. What are its coordinates?___, ___

   ☆ What was the name of the capital: _____

Driving Through Iowa

Standards

Students will

- Write in a variety of forms of genres. (McREL 1)
- Use maps to get information. (McREL 6)
- Access information efficiently and effectively. (AASL/AECT 1)
- Evaluate information critically and competently. (AASL/AECT 2)
- Use information effectively and creatively. (AASL/AECT 3)
- Strive for excellence in information seeking and knowledge generation. (AASL/AECT 6)
- Recognize the importance of information to a democratic society. (AASL/AECT 7)

Objectives

Students review and answer questions about map coordinates and landmarks.

Directions

1. The social studies teacher explains how latitude and longitude numbers make up a site's coordinates. The teacher points out the comparison of coordinates to the *Battleship* board game, in which coordinates are also used.

2. The library teacher introduces road maps and shows how to read them by looking at coordinates. The teacher also points out that a star shows the capital of a state.

3. Students read the Iowa map on the worksheet to answer questions about the state's landmarks and their coordinates.

4. As student pairs complete worksheets, teachers check for excellence in learning through understanding.

5. If time, students may look at another Iowa map and add other cities or landmarks to the worksheet map. Students may also add a compass rose.

Learning Styles

Linguistic (writing), mathematical (using computers), spatial (reading maps), and interpersonal (working in pairs).

Teaching Team

Library and social studies teachers.

Suggested Sources

Rand McNally. 2005 *Rand McNally Road Atlas: United States, Canada, & Mexico.* Skokie, IL: Rand McNally, 2005.

Acting Out Brer Rabbit

Brer Rabbit played tricks. Brer Fox played tricks too. Change a Brer Rabbit tale, like "Brer Rabbit and Tar Baby." Then make it into a short skit. Write the dialog:

Brer Rabbit: _____

Brer Fox: _____

_____

_____

_____

_____

_____

Acting Out Brer Rabbit

Standards

Students will

- Write in a variety of forms of genres. (McREL 1)
- Use reading skills and strategies to understand a variety of familiar literary passages and text (e.g., fairy tales, folktales, fiction, nonfiction, fables, legends, poems, biographies). (McREL 9)
- Know the elements that compose a story (e.g., character, plot, events, setting). (McREL 10)
- Appreciate and enjoy literature and other creative expressions of information. (AASL/AECT 5)
- Participate effectively in groups to pursue and generate information. (AASL/AECT 9)

Objectives

Students listen to a Brer Rabbit folktale. After discussing plot, setting, main characters, and a different ending or plot, students create a dialog for a skit.

Directions

1. This lesson takes two class sessions.
2. The library teacher explains that Brer Rabbit has a rich African heritage reaching back hundreds of years. The teacher tells a short Brer Rabbit folktale.
3. Students explain the folktale plot, setting, and main characters. They also explain how they might change the folktale. For example, how would they change the ending?
4. The language arts teacher directs various small student groups as they create a dialog for the Brer Rabbit skit, including some story changes.
5. During art class, the teacher helps students create skit props. During the next library class, student groups use their scripts to act out their story out with the props.

Learning Styles

Linguistic (writing), spatial (creating), bodily kinesthetic (acting), mathematical (thinking logically), and interpersonal (working together).

Teaching Team

Art, language arts, and library teachers.

Suggested Sources

Hamilton, Virginia. *Bruh Rabbit and the Tar Baby Girl.* New York: Scholastic, 2003.
Harris, Joel. *Brer Rabbit and The Wonderful Tar Baby.* Edina, MN: Abdo and Daughters, 2004.
Lester, Julius. *The Tales of Uncle Remus. The Adventures of Brer Rabbit.* New York: Puffin, 1997.

Science Book Parts

A textbook such as a science book has many parts to help you find and understand things in the book. This science book has the following parts:

Title Page   Copyright Page   Index

Glossary   Table of Contents

Fill in the blanks using the words above:

1. How do you find the meanings of science words in the science book? Use the _____

2. There is a place in the back of the science book that shows the pages of topics or subjects in ABC order. What is it called? _____

3. The page that shows when the science book was published is called the

    _____

4. Which page shows the title, author, and publisher?_____

5. To find a certain chapter look it up in the _____

From Joyce Keeling, *Lesson Plans for the Busy Librarian: A Standards Based Approach for the Elementary Library Media Center*, Volume 2. Westport, CT: Libraries Unlimited. © 2006.

Science Book Parts

Standards

Students will

- Use the various parts of a book. (McREL 11)
- Pursue information related to personal interests. (AASL/AECT 4)
- Strive for excellence in information seeking and knowledge generation. (AASL/AECT 6)

Objectives

Students define and use the title page, table of contents, copyright page, glossary, and index book parts.

Directions

1. The library teacher shows the book parts of library books: title page, table of contents, copyright page, glossary, and index.
2. The language arts teacher lists the book parts, and then writes their definitions on the board as students defines them. For example, students might say that the glossary is like a dictionary, or they may say that an index is something that shows subjects of importance in a book.
3. Students answer the worksheet questions, using their science books in order to develop a better understanding of book parts.
4. Students use the science book index and table of contents to find two different facts. They write the facts on the back of their worksheets. The science teacher assists.
5. Students finally complete the flower maze on their worksheet.

Learning Styles

Linguistic (reading and writing), spatial (doing puzzles), interpersonal (working in groups), and intrapersonal (working alone).

Teaching Team

Library, language arts, and science teachers.

Suggested Sources

Any books with a glossary and table of contents.
Student science books.

Where Can You Find It?

(1) Form teams! (2) After hearing each of the following questions, the team will hold up the E (for encyclopedia) or the D (for dictionary) once it has decided whether to use an encyclopedia or to use a dictionary to answer the question.

1. Who won World War I?	10. What is the meaning of *gilt*?
2. Who is Tiger Woods?	11. What is a short definition of *drone*?
3. How do you describe *lunge*?	12. What did Henry Ford invent?
4. What did Babe Ruth do?	13. What is the definition of *gnat*?
5. How is a pearl made?	14. What are some desert animals?
6. What is luck?	15. What's the meaning of A.M.?
7. How do you say *shish kebab*	16. How do you spell *fabricate*?
8. Where are diamonds found?	17. How does a rocket work?
9. What's a short definition of *pa*?	18. How do you spell *facilitate*?

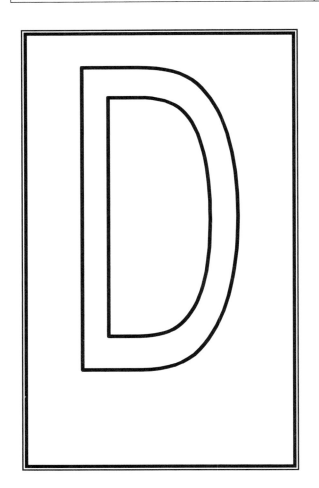 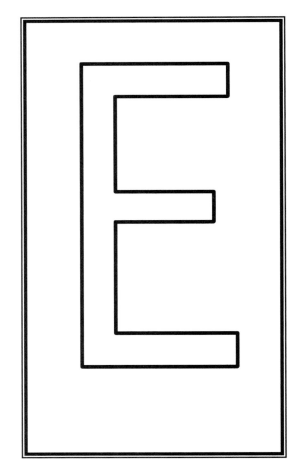

Where Can You Find It?

Standards

Students will

- Use encyclopedias to gather information. (McREL 2)
- Use a variety of resource materials to gather information for research topics (e.g., magazines, newspapers, dictionaries, schedules, journals, phone directories, globes, atlases, and almanacs). (McREL 7)
- Access information efficiently and effectively. (AASL/AECT 1)
- Practice ethical behavior in regard to information and information technology. (AASL/AECT 8)
- Participate effectively in groups to pursue and generate information. (AASL/AECT 9)

Objectives

Student teams review when to use a dictionary and when to use an encyclopedia in a relay game.

Directions

1. Copy the worksheet onto a different color of paper for each team.
2. The library and language arts teachers host an Encyclopedia/Dictionary Relay.
3. The library teacher reminds students when to use an encyclopedia and when to use a dictionary. For example, dictionaries are used to define, spell, pronounce, give meanings of words, and so on. Encyclopedias are used to give more information on people, places, and things.
4. Student's form and name teams. Each team will have a "D" and an "E."
5. Teachers ask the worksheet questions, and teams answer as quickly as possible with the letter for the correct reference book answer, holding up a D for dictionary and an E for encyclopedia. Two students will watch and keep points for the first team whose members raise their hands and answer correctly.
6. Once the Encyclopedia/Dictionary Relay is over, student worksheets are given to the teams. Teams are timed as they write short definitions of as many dictionary words as possible.

Learning Styles

Linguistic (finding answers), mathematical (thinking logically), and interpersonal (working in teams).

Teaching Team

Library and language arts teachers.

Suggested Sources

Any available dictionaries and encyclopedias.

Space Missions

For successful missions while searching encyclopedias, use these steps:

1st: Find the correct volume.

2nd: Skim guidewords.

3rd: Read the entry. The entry has your information!

Mission 1: Look up any word about space in the encyclopedia.

1. What is your search word (keyword)? _____

2. Which encyclopedia volume are you using? _____

3. What are the guidewords on the page that has your entry? _____

4. Write one fact from your entry (watch out—don't plagiarize!): _____

_____

Mission 2: Look up another word about space in the encyclopedia.

1. What is your search word (keyword)? _____

2. Which encyclopedia volume are you using? _____

3. What are the guidewords on the page that has your entry? _____

4. Write one fact from your entry (watch out—don't plagiarize!): _____

_____

Space Missions

Standards

Students will

- Write in a variety of genres. (McREL 1)
- Use encyclopedias to gather information for research purposes. (McREL 2)
- Use key words, guidewords, alphabetical and numerical order, indexes, cross references, and letters on volumes to find information for research. (McREL 5)
- Access information efficiently and effectively. (AASL/AECT 1)
- Use information effectively and creatively. (AASL/AECT 3)
- Pursue information related to personal interests. (AASL/AECT 4)
- Practice ethical behavior in regard to information and information technology. (AASL/AECT 8)
- Participate effectively in groups to pursue and generate information. (AASL/AECT 9)

Objectives

Students use encyclopedias to research space topics by using the three steps of successful encyclopedia searching.

Directions

1. The library teacher shows students the three steps of successful encyclopedia searching. The steps to successful results are first, to find the correct volume; second, to skim the guidewords; and third, to read the entry carefully.
2. The science teacher has students brainstorm different space terms, such as planets, galaxies, stars, space missions, and so on. The teacher shows students how to find information using the three steps of successful encyclopedia searching.
3. On their worksheets, small student groups write two space words as their keywords or search words.
4. Student groups complete the worksheet questions after searching encyclopedias.
5. Students share their facts with the class.

Learning Styles

Linguistic (writing, reading) and interpersonal (working in groups).

Teaching Team

Library and science teachers.

Suggested Sources

World Book. *World Book Encyclopedia*. Chicago, IL: World Book, 2005.

The Milkmaid and Her Pail

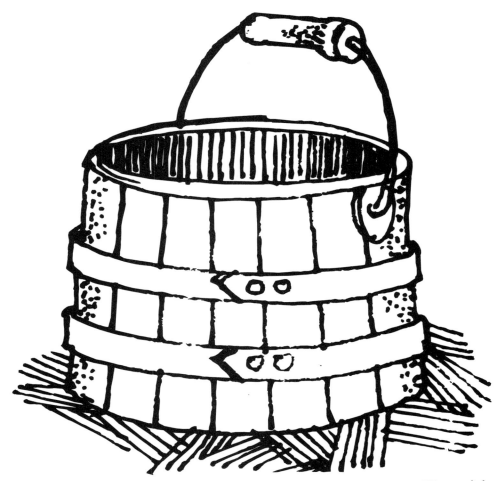

As she balanced her milk in a bucket on her head, a milkmaid walked down the road dreaming of all the things she could buy from the sale of her milk. She soon forgot about her bucket of milk on her head.

1. What happened to her milk?

2. Why is the moral of the fable, "Don't count your chickens before they hatch?"

3. Write down one or two personal wishes on these two slips of paper. Then attach your wishes to the back of the bucket.

From Joyce Keeling, *Lesson Plans for the Busy Librarian: A Standards Based Approach for the Elementary Library Media Center*, Volume 2. Westport, CT: Libraries Unlimited. © 2006.

The Milkmaid and Her Pail

Standards

Students will

- Write in a variety of forms of genre. (McREL 1)
- Use reading skills and strategies to understand a variety of familiar literary passages and text (e.g., fairy tales, folktales, fiction, nonfiction, fables, legends, poems, biographies). (McREL 9)
- Know the elements that compose a story (e.g., character, plot, events, setting). (McREL 10)
- Appreciate and enjoy literature and other creative expressions of information. (AASL/AECT 5)
- Recognize the importance of information to a democratic society. (AASL/AECT 7)
- Participate effectively in groups to pursue and generate information. (AASL/AECT 9)

Objectives

Students listen to and discuss the plot, character, and moral of a fable. Students answer worksheet questions about the fable, and then write two wishes.

Directions

1. The library teacher discusses fable elements, such as fables having morals.
2. The language arts teacher reads or tells the "The Milkmaid" fable.
3. After hearing the fable, students discuss its plot, character, and moral.
4. Small student groups discuss the worksheet questions and answer the questions.
5. Students color the milk bucket.
6. Since the milkmaid had some wishes, students write two of their own wishes on the small slips of paper. Wishes are taped to the back of the pail.
7. If desired, students may share their wishes with the class.

Learning Styles

Linguistic (reading, writing), spatial (coloring, imagining), interpersonal (working in groups), and intrapersonal (writing wishes).

Teaching Team

Language arts and reading teachers.

Suggested Sources

McCarthy, Tara. *Multicultural Fables and Fairy Tales*. New York: Scholastic, 1999.
Pinkney, Jerry. "The Milkmaid and Her Pail." *Aesop's Fables*. New York: SeaStar Books, 2000.

Going for the Goal!

(1) See how many different kinds of things to read are found in a magazine and then a newspaper. Are they different or alike? (2) Fill in the soccer ball areas by writing in the things to read from each place. How will you score?

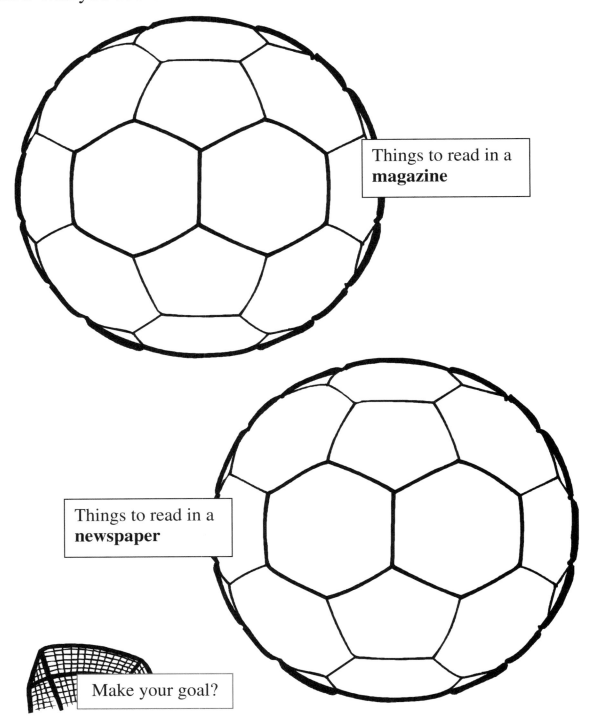

Things to read in a **magazine**

Things to read in a **newspaper**

Make your goal?

Going for the Goal!

Standards

Students will

- Use a variety of resource materials to gather information for research topics (e.g., magazines, newspapers, dictionaries, schedules, journals, phone directories, globes, atlases, and almanacs). (McREL 7)
- Know the difference between fact and fiction, real and make-believe. (McREL 8)
- Access information efficiently and effectively. (AASL/AECT 1)
- Evaluate information critically and competently. (AASL/AECT 2)
- Use information effectively and creatively. (AASL/AECT 3)
- Strive for excellence in information seeking and knowledge generation. (AASL/AECT 6)
- Recognize the importance of information to a democratic society. (AASL/AECT 7)

Objectives

Students browse, write, and compare things to read in magazines and newspapers.

Directions

1. The library teacher shows students the magazines that are available in their library. Teachers show and discuss things found in a magazine, like fiction stories, nonfiction articles (used for research), puzzles, games, and so on.
2. The social studies teacher shows the newspapers available in their library. Teachers show and discuss things found in a newspaper, such as editorials, comics, sports sections, business sections, and so on.
3. Student pairs select a magazine and a newspaper. They browse each source and list things to read in the soccer ball spaces on their worksheet.
4. Teachers check students' progress.
5. Teachers check to see which student pairs filled in the most soccer ball spaces. Answers are written in two lists or in a Venn diagram on the board.

Learning Styles

Mathematical (thinking logically), spatial (thinking visually), linguistic (writing), interpersonal, and intrapersonal (working alone).

Teaching Team

Library and social studies teachers.

Suggested Sources

Any newspapers.

Any elementary magazines, such as *American Girl, Boy's Life, Cobblestone, Kids Discover, Sports Illustrated for Kids, Odyssey, Zoobooks, Faces,* and others.

Finding Facts Around the World

Use *The Scholastic Kid's Almanac for the 21st Century* or *The World Almanac For Kids 2005* to find these facts about the world.

1. What is the population of the country of China? Look under the World Geography or the Nations section. _____

2. Who is on the $100.00 bill? Look under Business and Money or Money and Business._____

3. Which NFL football player career rusher was the top or record holder fieldrusher? Look under the Sports section._____

4. What is the world's tallest or highest mountain? Look under the Geography section. _____

5. What is the best-selling video? Look under the Television and Movies (Movies) section. _____

6. What is the weight of the blue whale, the largest or biggest marine animal (mammal)? Look under the Animals section. _____

Bonus Question. Find two computer facts:

1. _____

2. _____

Finding Facts Around the World

Standards

Students will

- Write in a variety of genre. (McREL 1)
- Use a variety of resource materials to gather information for research topics (e.g., magazines, newspapers, dictionaries, schedules, journals, phone directories, globes, atlases, and almanacs). (McREL 7)
- Access information efficiently and effectively. (AASL/AECT 1)
- Evaluate information critically and competently. (AASL/AECT 2)
- Use information effectively and creatively. (AASL/AECT 3)
- Participate effectively in groups to pursue and generate information. (AASL/AECT 9)

Objectives

Small student groups use a children's almanac and its table of contents.

Directions

1. The library teacher introduces *The Scholastic Kid's Almanac for the 21st Century* or *The World Almanac for Kids 2005* by explaining that these almanacs have graphs and charts to show facts, whereas regular almanacs give mostly written facts. (Note: The versions of the two almanac sources may change dramatically by copyright).
2. The language arts teacher explains that in order to answer the questions on their worksheets, students must use the table of contents to find the correct chapter sections. Students are told that each question has different hints.
3. Students write the worksheet answers, as their small groups finds the answers.
4. As soon as a group completes the worksheets, the class compares answers.
5. If time permits, students may browse regular almanacs.
6. In art class, students color and laminate the world picture from their worksheets. Then they punch a hole in the picture and add yarn for a key chain.

Learning Styles

Linguistic (reading, writing), spatial (reading maps and charts), interpersonal (working in groups), and intrapersonal (writing).

Teaching Team

Art, language arts, and library teachers.

Suggested Sources

Pascoe, Elaine and Deborah Kops. *Scholastic Kid's Almanac for the 21st Century*. New York: Scholastic, 1999.

Seabrooke, Kevin (ed.). *The World Almanac for Kids 2005*. New York: St. Martin's Press, 2005.

Little Match Girl

Little Match Girl

1. The main character in the story could be described as_____

2. Tell the main plot in one sentence:_____

_____

3. The theme of the story is _____

_____

4. How would you have changed the story?_____

_____

Little Match Girl

Standards

Students will

- Write in a variety of forms of genre. (McREL 1).
- Use reading skills and strategies to understand a variety of familiar literary passages and text (e.g., fairy tales, folktales, fiction, nonfiction, fables, legends, poems, biographies). (McREL 9)
- Know the elements that compose a story. (e.g., characters, plot, events, setting). (McREL 10)
- Appreciate and enjoy literature and other creative expressions of information. (AASL/AECT 5)
- Participate effectively in groups to pursue and generate information. (AASL/AECT 9)

Objectives

Students listen to *The Little Match Girl* and discuss its theme, main character, and main plot. Students make plate covers for light switches.

Directions

1. The library teacher reads or tells the story of *The Little Match Girl*, while pointing out what makes it a fairy tale.
2. The reading teacher explains that the *theme* is the purpose of a story—why the author wrote the story—and what one learns from the story. The class then explains the elements of this story: main character, main plot, and theme.
3. The class discusses how they could have changed the story.
4. Students fill out their worksheets.
5. Students write a motivational or inspirational saying in the box under the Match Girl that relates to the theme. For instance, they may write "Help Others."
6. Students cut out around the outside of the Match Girl and around the small box in the middle of her. The Match Girl is a light switch cover, and a story reminder.

Learning Styles

Linguistic (writing), mathematical (thinking logically), spatial (creating), intrapersonal (working alone), and interpersonal (discussing).

Teaching Team

Library and reading team.

Suggested Sources

Isadora, Rachel. *Little Match Girl.* New York: G.P. Putnam Sons, 1990.
Mattheas, Andrew. *Stories From Hans Christian Anders*en. New York: Orchard, 1993.
Pinkney, Jerry [Retold]. *The Little Match Girl.* New York: Puffin, 1999.
Rowe, Gavin. *Fairy Tales.* Newmarket, England: Brimax, 1996.

Deck the Halls

Use these ornaments to show your favorite fiction and nonfiction books! Write the titles, authors, and call numbers. Then decorate!

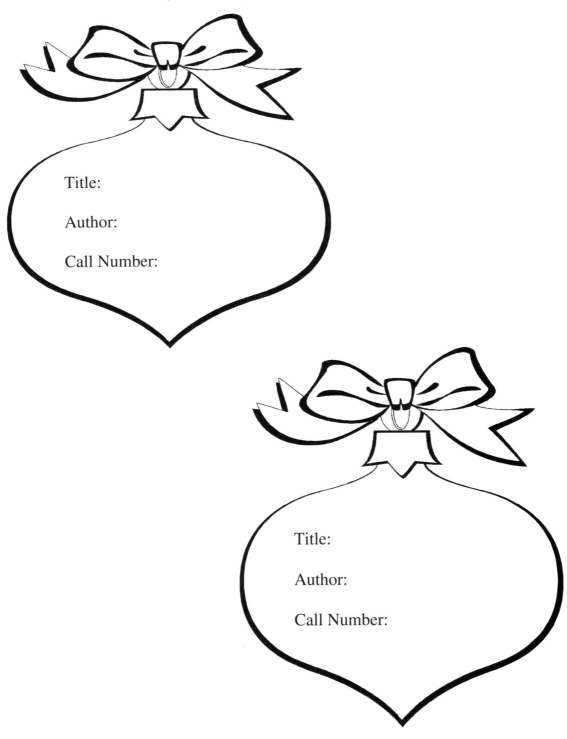

Title:

Author:

Call Number:

Title:

Author:

Call Number:

Deck the Halls

Standards

Students will

- Write in a variety of forms of genre. (McREL 1)
- Use library catalog. (McREL 3)
- Know the difference between fact and fiction, real and make-believe.(McREL 8)
- Pursue information related to personal interests. (AASL/AECT 4)
- Appreciate and enjoy literature and other creative expressions of information. (AASL/AECT 5)

Objectives

Students write about a favorite fiction and nonfiction book on paper Christmas ornaments.

Directions

1. Copy the student worksheet on sheets of festive construction paper.
2. The library teacher reviews the differences between fiction and nonfiction with the students.
3. Students browse library shelves or the card catalog for favorite fiction and nonfiction books. The library and reading teachers help students recall their favorite books.
4. Teachers assist students as they write their favorite book titles, authors, and the call numbers on the ornaments.
5. Students decorate the outer rim of their ornaments.
6. Students decorate or "deck" the library tree with the ornaments in order to get other students interested in their favorite books.

Learning Styles

Linguistic (writing), spatial (creating, coloring), and intrapersonal (working alone).

Teaching Team

Library and reading teachers.

Suggested Sources

Favorite nonfiction and fiction books.

It's Kwanzaa Time!

 **Kwanzaa!**

Black, green, and red are symbols of Kwanzaa. What do they mean?

Green:

Red:

Black

During Kwanzaa, gifts are given. It's also a time to make mats. Make a coaster mat for a juice glass. Give it as a gift. Color the strips green, red, and black.

Leave the joined strips together, cutting on the dotted lines. Cut out the single strips and weave them in and out of the joined strips.

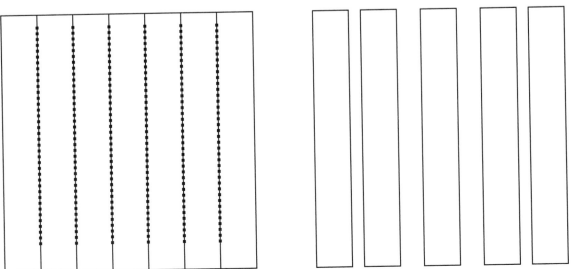

It's Kwanzaa Time!

Standards

Students will

- Write in a variety of forms of genres. (McREL 1)
- Use electronic media to gather information (Internet, videos). (McREL 4)
- Use reading skills and strategies to understand a variety of familiar literary passages and text (e.g., fairy tales, folktales, fiction, nonfiction, fables, legends, poems, biographies). (McREL 9)
- Evaluate information critically and competently. (AASL/AECT 2)
- Use information effectively and creatively. (AASL/AECT 3)
- Recognize the importance of information to a democratic society. (AASL/AECT 7)

Objectives

Students answer questions on Kwanzaa. They weave a juice coaster.

Directions

1. The social studies teacher defines Kwanzaa as simply as possible, while explaining that it is observed between December 26th and January 1st.
2. The library teacher reads one or two books about Kwanzaa. The symbolism of the red, black, and green colors is explained.
3. Students write one of the definitions of the color symbolism after the Kwanzaa colors of red (blood shed), black (skin color), and green (mother land and hope).
4. Teachers explain that weaving is a Kwanzaa tradition. Students color and then weave a small placemat-type juice coaster in red, black, and green.
5. The art teacher helps with the weaving. The juice coasters are laminated. Students may make paper chains out of the same Kwanzaa colors to decorate the room.
6. Students may learn more about the holiday using the Internet.

Learning Styles

Linguistic (writing), spatial (creating), and intrapersonal (working alone).

Teaching Team

Art, social studies, and library teachers.

Suggested Sources

Grier, Ella. *Seven Days of Kwanzaa*. New York: Viking, 1997.
Medeans, Angela. *Shelf: Seven Spools of Thread*. New York: Albert Whitman and Co., 2000.
Pinkney, Andrea Davis. *Seven Candles for Kwanzaa*. New York: Dial, 1993.
Washington, Donna C. *The Story of Kwanzaa*. New York: HarperTrophy, 1997.
World Book. *World Book Encyclopedia*. Chicago, IL: World Book, 2005.
This Internet site has Kwanzaa facts and ideas: http://www.kidsdomain.com/holiday/kwanzaa

Diving for Shark Bites of Information

   (1) Dive into the Internet to find and write 5 facts about sharks.
(2) Color the shark and its ocean. (3) Make a freestanding shark display!
Fold on the dotted lines as directed. (4) Cut on the following solid line.

Sharks by: _____

Fold this line in.↑

   1. _____

   2. _____

   3. _____

   4. _____

   5. _____

The Internet site used: _____

Fold this line out. ↕

Diving for Shark Bites of Information

Standards

Students will

- Write in a variety of forms of genre. (McREL 1)
- Use electronic media to gather information (e.g., Internet, videos). (McREL 4)
- Access information efficiently and effectively. (AASL/AECT 1)
- Evaluate information critically and competently. (AASL/AECT 2)
- Use information effectively and creatively. (AASL/AECT 3)
- Practice ethical behavior in regard to information and information technology. (AASL/AECT 8)
- Participate effectively in groups to pursue and generate information. (AASL/AECT 9)

Objectives

Using the Internet, students research sharks and write five facts. They color and make a freestanding shark display.

Directions

1. The language arts and library teachers introduce Internet sites on sharks.
2. Teachers help student pairs use the Internet to locate shark facts. Students write five shark facts of their choice on their worksheets.
3. Students are reminded to write neatly, as their work will be displayed.
4. Students write the Internet address used to find their facts.
5. Students color their worksheet sharks and add a colorful ocean scene to their shark display.
6. Students cut and fold their displays creating a freestanding shark display.

Learning Styles

Linguistic (reading, writing), interpersonal (working in groups), mathematical (using computers), and intrapersonal (writing).

Teaching Team

Language arts and library teachers.

Suggested Sources

Internet sites containing shark information:

http://www.enchantedlearning.com
http://www.kidzone.ws
http://www.nationalgeographic.com/kid
http://www.npca.org/marine_and_coastal/marine_wildlife/sharks.asp
http://www.seaworld.org

Great Words

What did Martin Luther King Say?

Speech Notes:

_____

_____

_____

_____

_____

_____

_____

_____

_____

_____

_____

_____

Great Words

Standards

Students will

- Write in a variety of forms of genre. (McREL 1)
- Use reading skills and strategies to understand a variety of familiar literary passages and text (e.g., fairy tales, folktales, fiction, nonfiction, fables, legends, poems, biographies). (McREL 9)
- Evaluate information critically and competently. (AASL/AECT 2)
- Use information effectively and creatively. (AASL/AECT 3)
- Pursue information related to personal interests. (AASL/AECT 4)
- Recognize the importance of information to a democratic society. (AASL/AECT 7)

Objectives

After researching and hearing about Martin Luther King, Jr., students give a speech.

Directions

1. This lesson takes two class periods.
2. The social studies teacher describes Martin Luther King, Jr. and reads either a short passage or a short easy book on him.
3. The library teacher introduces Martin Luther King nonfiction sources.
4. Students research Martin Luther King and write a short 1–2 minute speech on his beliefs. Students write their speech notes in the narrow worksheet areas.
5. Students portray themselves as Martin Luther King when they give their speech.
6. During the next class time, students give their speeches. They may either tape the worksheet tie on themselves while giving the speech, or use it as a speech note cover.

Learning Styles

Linguistic (writing), bodily kinesthetic (acting), and intrapersonal (working alone).

Teaching Team

Library and social studies teachers.

Suggested Sources

Adler, David. *Picture Book of Martin Luther King, Jr.* New York: Holiday House, 1989.

Feeney, Kathy. *Martin Luther King, Jr.: Photo-Illustrated Biography.* Mankato, MN.: Bridgestone Press, 2002.

Koslow, Philip and Rachel Kranz. *The Biographical Dictionary of African-Americans.* New York: Checkmark Books, 1999.

Mattern, Joanne. *Young Martin Luther King, Jr.: I Have a Dream.* Mahwah, New Jersey, 1992.

Hear Ye, Hear Ye!

Robin Hood has been seen! Describe what you have heard! Write it in an acrostic poem using the letters of Robin Hood's name.

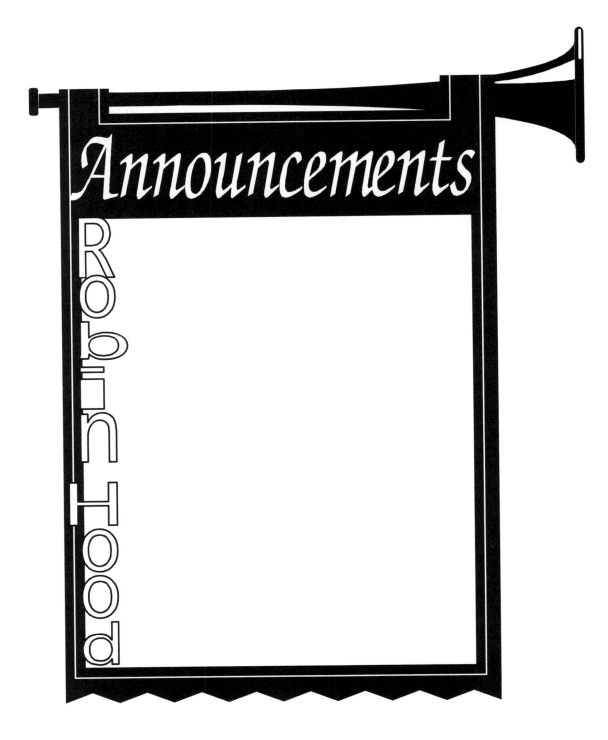

Hear Ye, Hear Ye!

Standards

Students will

- Write in a variety of genres. (McREL 1)
- Use reading skills and strategies to understand a variety of familiar literary passages and text (e.g., fairy tales, folktales, fiction, nonfiction, fables, legends, poems, biographies). (McREL 9)
- Appreciate and enjoy literature and other creative expressions of information. (AASL/AECT 5)
- Participate effectively in groups to pursue and generate information. (AASL/AECT 9)

Objectives

Students discuss the plot and main characters of a Robin Hood legend. They write an acrostic poem about the story.

Directions

1. The library teacher gives a very brief background of Robin Hood and then reads a short Robin Hood story. The teacher points out why the story is a legend.
2. After hearing the story, the reading teacher has students explain the main plot and main characters.
3. Students create an acrostic poem about the Robin Hood story on their worksheet banners.
4. Students hang up their banners and attach ribbons.
5. In music class, students can sing a Robin Hood ballad.

Learning Styles

Linguistic (writing), musical (rhyming), interpersonal (working together), and intrapersonal (working alone).

Teaching Team

Library, reading, and music teachers.

Suggested Sources

Makolmson, Anne. *The Song of Robin Hood.* New York: Houghton Mifflin, 2000. [Ballads]
Osborne, Mary Pope. *Favorite Medieval Tales.* New York: Scholastic, 1999.
Willey, Bee. *The Golden Hoard.* New York: Margaret K. McElderry Books, 1996.
World Book. "The Shooting Match." In *Childcraft: The How and Why Library.* Chicago, IL: World Book, 2005.
Yolen, Jane. *Sherwood.* New York: Philomel, 2000.

Pied Piper Money

1. What is the beginning plot of the Pied Piper story?

2. What is the main plot of the story?

3. What is the ending plot of the story?

Here is a bookmark of the story:

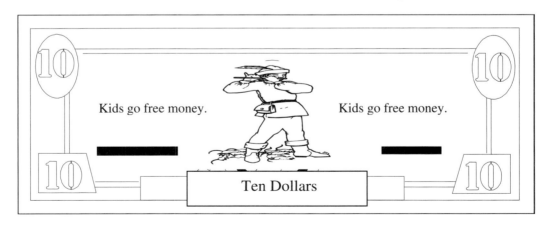

Kids go free money.   Kids go free money.

Ten Dollars

From Joyce Keeling, *Lesson Plans for the Busy Librarian: A Standards Based Approach for the Elementary Library Media Center*, Volume 2. Westport, CT: Libraries Unlimited. © 2006.

Pied Piper Money

Standards

Students will

- Write in a variety of forms of genres. (McREL 1)
- Use reading skills and strategies to understand a variety of familiar literary passages and text. (McREL 9)
- Know the elements that compose a story. (e.g., character, plot, events, setting). (McREL 10)
- Appreciate and enjoy literature and other creative expressions of information. (AASL/AECT 5)
- Strive for excellence in information seeking and knowledge generation. (AASL/AECT 6)
- Participate effectively in groups to pursue and generate information. (AASL/AECT 9)

Objectives

Students listen to and then discuss the plots of *The Pied Piper*. They make a bookmark.

Directions

1. The reading teacher reads *The Pied Piper* story while explaining that it's a fairy tale.
2. After the students hear the story, the library teacher has students explain the beginning, middle, and ending story plots. Then students answer the worksheet questions.
3. Students color and cut out the money bookmarks after the teachers have checked to ensure that all students have successfully answered the questions.

Learning Styles

Mathematical (thinking logically), linguistic (writing), interpersonal (working together), and intrapersonal (working alone).

Teaching Team

Library and reading teachers.

Suggested Sources

Helmer, Marilyn. *Three Tuneful Tales*. Toronto, Canada: Kids Can Press, 2003.
Holden, Robert. *The Pied Piper of Hamelin*. Boston, MA: Houghton Mifflin, 1998.

How Did a Native American Live?

Research a Native American tribe. On the first tepee write the name of the tribe and decorate it. On the second tepee, describe the dwelling the tribe used (it may not be a tepee) and where the tribe lived in North America. On the third and fourth tepees write more facts.

How Did a Native American Live?

Standards

Students will

- Use electronic media to gather information (e.g., Internet, videos). (McREL 4)
- Use reading skills and strategies to understand a variety of familiar literary passages and forms of text (e.g., fairy tales, folktales, fiction, nonfiction, fables, legends, poems, biographies). (McREL 9)
- Access information efficiently and effectively. (AASL/AECT 1)
- Evaluate information critically and competently. (AASL/AECT 2)
- Use information effectively and creatively. (AASL/AECT 3)
- Recognize the importance of information to a democratic society. (AASL/AECT 7)
- Practice ethical behavior in regard to information and information technology. (AASL/AECT 8)

Objectives

Student pairs research a Native American tribe and make tepee fact booklets.

Directions

1. The social studies teacher assigns student pairs a Native American tribe. Students write the name of their tribes on the cover, the first worksheet tepee.
2. The library teacher guides students' research on a tribe, using nonfiction books or Internet. Students write brief facts and avoid plagiarism.
3. On the second tepee, students explain the tribe's dwelling and geographic location. On the third and fourth tepees, they write other facts such as food or customs.
4. Students cut out the tepees, and attach the two sets of tepees together to make one folding tepee booklet. They decorate the booklet cover.
5. Teachers may extend the lesson and have students find more facts.

Learning Styles

Linguistic (writing), spatial (creating), and intrapersonal (working alone).

Teaching Team

Library and social studies teachers.

Suggested Sources

Lassieur, Allison. *The Cheyenne*. Mankato, MN: Bridgestone Press, 2001.
Levine, Ellen. *If You Lived With the Iroquois ...* New York: Scholastic, 1998.
Oskinski, Alice. *The Sioux*. Chicago: Children's Press, 1984.
Sneve, Virginia Driving Hawk. *The Nez Perce*. New York: Holiday House, 1994.
Sneve, Virgina Driving Hawk. *The Seminoles*. New York: Holiday House, 1994.
Internet site containing information on Native American history for kids:
http://www.kidinfo.com/American_History/Native_Americans.html

Springing into April

Springing into April

Use the Card Catalog to Search

1. Search for a book about Spring:

Subject:_____Spring_____   Title:_____

Call Number:_____   Author:_____

                                       Copyright:_____

2. Search for a book on something fun that you could do in the Spring:

(for example kites, bikes, basketball, skating):

Subject:_____   Title:_____

Call Number:_____   Author:_____

                                       Copyright:_____

3. Search for a joke or riddle book:

Subject:_____   Title:_____

Call Number:_____   Author:_____

                                       Copyright:_____

   *Find the joke or riddle book!

4. Write a very short riddle from the joke or riddle book. Then staple one end
    of the April Fool's word box over the riddle or joke answer

_____

_____

_____

_____

April **Fools!**

From Joyce Keeling, *Lesson Plans for the Busy Librarian: A Standards Based Approach for the Elementary Library Media Center*, Volume 2. Westport, CT: Libraries Unlimited. © 2006.

Springing into April

Standards

Students will

- Write in a variety of forms of genre. (McREL 1)
- Use the library catalog. (McREL 3)
- Access information efficiently and effectively. (AASL/AECT 1)
- Strive for excellence in information seeking and knowledge generation. (AASL/AECT 6)
- Participate effectively in groups to pursue and generate information. (AASL/AECT 9)

Objectives

Students use the automated card catalog to locate spring books. They read the card catalog entries and write down the call number, title, author, copyright, and subject.

Directions

1. The library teacher uses the automated card catalog with an overhead LCD projector to project and review subject, title, and author searching methods. The teacher shows how to read an automated catalog card or record for call number, title, author, copyright, and subject.
2. The language arts teacher has students brainstorm April or springtime topics.
3. Small student groups use the card catalog to find April topics and write the call number, author, title, copyright, and subject of the books they find.
4. Teachers examine students' work for exemplary understanding.
5. When searching is completed, students locate a joke or riddle book and write an April Fool's joke. After the joke is written, the paper April Fool's box flap is placed over the joke or riddle answer.

Learning Styles

Linguistic (reading and writing), mathematical (using card catalog computers), bodily kinesthetic (using the card catalog), intrapersonal (writing), and interpersonal (working in groups).

Teaching Team

Library and science teachers.

Suggested Sources

Card catalog.

Solving a Case

Solve a case! Draw or write *a few words* to solve it

Case File
Who was there?

Case File
Where did it happen?

Case File
What happened?

Case File
Solve it!

Case Closed! Case Title (Book Title):
Investigator (Your Name):

Solving a Case

Standards

Students will

- Write in a variety of forms of genre. (McREL 1)
- Know the elements that compose a story (e.g., character, plot, events, setting). (McREL 10)
- Appreciate and enjoy literature and other creative expressions of information. (AASL/AECT 5)

Objectives

Students listen to a short mystery book, and answer worksheet questions to try to solve the mystery. The main plot, characters, and setting of the mystery are discussed.

Directions

1. The reading and library teachers take turns reading a short mystery to the class.
2. Students are told to think like a detective to solve the mystery. First, students write their names at the bottom of their sheets as investigators. They jot notes around the outside of their worksheets until given the opportunity to answer each question.
3. Students only answer a question when it has a direct relationship to the mystery (or crime). In Case File #1, students list the main characters of the mystery, in Case File #2 they write the setting of the mystery, and in Case File #3 they write the main mystery plot. If some students would rather draw than write the answers, they may do so.
4. In the last Case File, students attempt to solve the mystery before hearing the ending or the solution.
5. Finally, students write the book title.

Learning Styles

Linguistic (writing), mathematical (thinking with strategies), and intrapersonal (working alone).

Teaching Team

Library and reading teachers.

Suggested Sources

Adler, David. *Cam Jansen and the Mystery of the Haunted House*. New York: Puffin, 1999.
Paulsen, Gary. *Captive*. New York: Yearling, 1995.
Roy, Ron. *Haunted Hotel*. New York: Random House, 1999.
Roy, Ron. *The Orange Outlaw*. New York: Random House, 2001.
Wright, Betty Ren. *The Ghost Witch*. New York: Holiday House, 1993.

Mummies

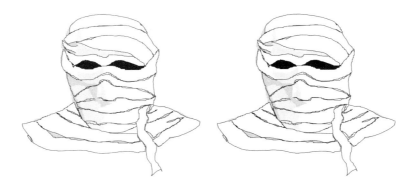

Unwrap the facts on mummies! What facts will you unravel?

1. Use an encyclopedia. Discover and write 1–2 facts on mummies.

_____

_____

Prove your findings! Write the encyclopedia bibliography:

Keyword:_____   Encyclopedia:_____

Volume:_____   Copyright: _____

Publisher:_____   Publishing Place: _____

2. Use a nonfiction book. Discover and write 1–2 more facts.

_____

_____

Prove your findings again. Write the book bibliography

Author: _____   Title:_____

Publishing Place:_____   Copyright: _____

Publisher:_____

Now, the mummies will become your pencil topper for a surprising twist!

Mummies

Standards

Students will

- Write in a variety of forms of genre. (McREL 1)
- Use encyclopedias to gather information for research topics. (McREL 2)
- Use library catalog. (McREL 3)
- Use reading skills and strategies to understand a variety of familiar literary passages and text (e.g., fairy tales, folktales, fiction, nonfiction, fables, legends, poems, biographies). (McREL 9)
- Access information efficiently and effectively. (AASL/AECT 1)
- Evaluate information critically and competently. (AASL/AECT 2)
- Use information effectively and creatively. (AASL/AECT 3)
- Strive for excellence in information seeking and knowledge generation. (AASL/AECT 6)
- Practice ethical behavior in regard to information and information technology. (AASL/AECT 8)

Objectives

Students find and write mummy facts from an encyclopedia and a nonfiction book. They write bibliographies. Students create mummy pencil toppers.

Directions

1. The social studies teacher guides students as they find and write mummy facts using an encyclopedia and a nonfiction book. Students are to write in their own words.
2. The library teacher shows students how to write encyclopedia and book bibliographies by the worksheet guidelines. Students' work is checked for understanding.
3. After successfully completing their worksheets, students cut out their worksheet mummy boxes. They fold the mummies in half and tape all the sides together, leaving the bottom open. They have a mummy pencil topper!

Learning Styles

Linguistic (writing) and intrapersonal (working alone).

Teaching Team

Library and social studies teachers.

Suggested Sources

Aliki. *Mummies Made in Egypt*. New York: HarperCollins, 1985.
Milton, Joyce. *Mummies*. New York: Grosset & Dunlap, 1996.
Putnam, James. *Eyewitness: Mummy*. New York: Dorling Kindersley 1993.
Ross, Dave. *Mummy Madness*. New York: Franklin, 1979. [Jokes]
Tanaka, Shelly. *Secrets of the Mummies*. New York: Hyperion Books, 2000.
World Book. *World Book Encyclopedia*. Chicago, IL: World Book, 2004.

Hound Dog Autographs

My Autograph Book

"Hounding You For Your Autograph"

From Joyce Keeling, *Lesson Plans for the Busy Librarian: A Standards Based Approach for the Elementary Library Media Center*, Volume 2. Westport, CT: Libraries Unlimited. © 2006.

Hound Dog Autographs

Standards

Students will

- Write in a variety of forms of genre. (McREL 1)
- Use reading skills and strategies to understand a variety of familiar literary passages and text (e.g., fairy tales, folktales, fiction, nonfiction, fables, legends, poems, biographies). (McREL 9)
- Pursue information related to personal interests. (AASL/AECT 4)
- Appreciate and enjoy literature and other creative expressions of information. (AASL/AECT 5)
- Participate effectively in groups to pursue and generate information. (AASL/AECT 9)

Objectives

Students find and write a riddle, joke, or autograph verse for their autograph books.

Directions

1. Students need extra copies of the bottom worksheet square for their books.
2. The library teacher reads autograph verses, riddles, or jokes that could be written in an autograph book. The teacher tells students that after making their autograph books, they will choose and write one verse, riddle, or joke in any direction in each other's books.
3. Students color and then cut out their worksheet autograph book covers. They'll add and staple extra blank pages to their autograph books.
4. Teachers guide students as students find a riddle, joke, or autograph verse.
5. Each student writes and then signs a verse, joke, or riddle in every classmate's autograph book, to provide a lasting reminder of third grade classmates.

Learning Styles

Linguistic (writing), musical (writing poems), intrapersonal (working alone), and interpersonal (working with other).

Teaching Team

Language arts and library teachers.

Suggested Sources

Horsfall, Jacqueline. *Gigantic Book of Riddles*. New York: Sterling, 2002.
Keller, John. *Awesome Jokes*. New York: Sterling Publishing, 1995.
Maestro, Giulio. *Razzle-Dazzle Riddles*. New York: Clarion Books, 1985.
Morrison, Lillian. *It Rained All Day That Night: Autographs, Rhymes & Inscriptions*. Little Rock, AR: August House, 2003.

Chapter 5
Fourth Grade Lesson Plans

A solid, professionally-based library lesson plan is built around developmental needs of students at their grade level, around the Kendall and Marzano or McREL National Education Language Arts Standards and Benchmarks, the AASL (American Association of School Libraries), and the AECT (Association for Educational Communications and Technology) Information Literacy Standards, and around the various learning styles of students as found in Gardner's Multiple Intelligences framework. (The selected AASL/AECT standards and Gardner's Multiple Intelligences are fully described in the introduction.) All of the following lessons are built around these standards, benchmarks, and skills in order to ensure that all students appreciate different forms of literature, and are competent users of information, and so become information literate.

Each lesson plan includes student objectives, team teaching suggestions, and suggested sources. Furthermore, each lesson is designed to last approximately twenty minutes. All lessons have been field-tested. The lessons provide individual or small-group worksheet work and are designed to make library learning enjoyable, to be easily accomplished in a librarian's or library teacher's busy schedule, and to be grounded in solid standards and benchmarks. Each lesson has a reference to the following McREL standards and benchmarks, as well as a reference to the AASL/AECT standards.

Fourth Grade Library Standards and Language Arts Benchmarks (McREL)

Reprinted by permission of McREL

Fourth grade students will be able to:

Use the general skills and strategies of the writing process. (Standard 1)

1. Write in a variety of genres. (Standard 1, Benchmark 7, under grades K–2)

Gather and use information for research purposes. (Standard 4)

2. Use encyclopedias to gather information. (Standard 4, Benchmark 2)
3. Use library catalog (Standard 4, Benchmark 2, under grades 6–8)
4. Use electronic media to gather information (e.g., Internet, videos). (Standard 4, Benchmark 4)
5. Use key words, guide words, alphabetical and numerical order, indexes, cross references, and letters on volumes to find information for research topics. (Standard 4, Benchmarks 5)
6. Use multiple representations of information (e.g., maps, charts, photos, diagrams, tables) to get information. (Standard 4, Benchmark 6)
7. Use a variety of resource materials to gather information for research topics (e.g., magazines, newspapers, dictionaries, schedules, journals, phone, directories, globes, atlases, and almanacs). (Standard 4, Benchmark 4, under grades 6–8)
8. Use strategies to gather information (e.g., notes). (Standard 4, Benchmark 7)

Use reading skills and strategies to understand and interpret a variety of literary texts. (Standard 6)

9. Use reading skills and strategies to understand a variety of familiar literary passages and text (e.g., fairy tales, folktales, fiction, nonfiction, fables, legends, poems, biographies). (Standard 6, Benchmark 1)
10. Know the elements that compose a story (e.g., character, plot, events, setting). (Standard 6, Benchmark 2, under Pre-K)

Use reading skills and strategies to understand and interpret a variety of informational texts. (Standard 7)

11. Use the various parts of a book. (Standard 7, Benchmark 4)

Card Catalog Team Challenge

Compete to see who has the fastest team players.

Team _____

(1) Use the card catalog. (2) Write the call number.

1. Find book title *The Guinness Book of World Records*. Call Number:

2. Find a fiction book by author Matt Christopher. Call Number:

3. Find any book of jokes. Call Number:

4. Find any poetry book. Call Number:

5. Find any nonfiction book on a sport. Call Number: Good Luck!

Now get the books!

Team _____

(1) Use the card catalog. (2) Write the call number.

1. Find book title *The Statue of Liberty*. Call Number:

2. Find a fiction book by author Gary Paulsen. Call Number:

3. Find any nonfiction book on snakes. Call Number:

4. Find any atlas. Call Number:

5. Find any book on Origami. Call Number: Good Luck!

Now get the books!

Card Catalog Team Challenge

Standards

Students will

- Use library catalog. (McREL 3)
- Access information efficiently and effectively. (AASL/AECT 1)
- Practice ethical behavior in regard to information and information technology. (AASL/AECT 8)
- Participate effectively in groups to pursue and generate information. (AASL/AECT 9)

Objectives

Student teams search the card catalog using author, title or subject searches.

Directions

1. The library teacher reviews how to use the card catalog, stressing title, author, and subject searches and how to use the call number. Students give examples of subject searching.
2. The language arts teacher organizes teams to search the card catalog, according to the number of card catalog stations.
3. Student teams create team names.
4. Teachers explain that teams will find the worksheet books on the card catalog and write down the complete call numbers. The first two questions are either title or author searches, but the last three questions are subject searches.
5. Teams locate the books after they have written all call numbers.
6. Student teams are timed to make the learning competition fun.

Learning Styles

Linguistic (writing), mathematical (using catalog computers), bodily kinesthetic (using the card catalog, finding books), and interpersonal (working with others)

Teaching Team

Language arts and library teachers

Suggested Sources

Library card catalog

Signals

Traffic lights guide people. Encyclopedia guidewords guide or signal people too. Guidewords are at the top of pages to show where keywords are located. In the encyclopedia, find the guidewords, page, and volume number for the following keywords.

Keyword	Guidewords	Page	Volume
1. Money	_____	_____	_____
2. Hurricane	_____	_____	_____
3. Otter	_____	_____	_____
4. Ship	_____	_____	_____
5. Gold	_____	_____	_____

There is another guide in the encyclopedia, the *cross-reference*. It tells you to look somewhere else. It may start with a "see" or "see also". Find and write the cross-reference words for the following keywords.

Keyword	Cross-Reference Words
1. Bicycle	_____
2. Skeleton	_____

Signals

Standards

Students will

- Write in a variety of genres. (McREL1)
- Use encyclopedias to gather information. (McREL 2)
- Use key words, guidewords, alphabetical and numerical order, indexes, cross-references, and letters on volumes to find information for research. (McREL 5)
- Access information efficiently and effectively. (AASL/AECT 1)
- Participate effectively in groups to pursue and generate information. (AASL/AECT 9)

Objectives

Student pairs or small groups use encyclopedia guidewords to find the volume and page numbers of given keywords. They also locate cross-reference words.

Directions

1. The library teacher explains that a cross reference can be prefaced by the words "see" or "see also," telling the reader to cross over to a different page and/or volume. The teacher shows some examples.
2. The language arts teacher explains how guidewords are used to locate words in an encyclopedia.
3. Student pairs or small groups use guidewords to locate the page and volume number of keyword searches in the encyclopedia. Then students locate two cross-reference words.
4. If time permits, students may look up the cross-referenced words and then write some facts.

Learning Styles

Linguistic (reading, writing) and interpersonal (working with others).

Teaching Team

Language arts and library teachers.

Suggested Sources

World Book. *World Book Encyclopedia*. Chicago, IL: World Book, 2005.

Desert Island Notes

Note Taking Notes:
1. Use the main idea.
2. Use very few words!
3. Use your own words.
4. Use supportive details.

Take notes on the island! Write your main idea on the sandy island base. Write your brief supporting details on the leaves of the tree.

From Joyce Keeling, *Lesson Plans for the Busy Librarian: A Standards Based Approach for the Elementary Library Media Center*, Volume 2. Westport, CT: Libraries Unlimited. © 2006.

Desert Island Notes

Standards

Students will

- Write in a variety of genres. (McREL 1)
- Use card catalog. (McREL 3).
- Use strategies to gather information (e.g., notes). (McREL 8)
- Access information efficiently and effectively. (AASL/AECT 1)
- Evaluate information critically and competently. (AASL/AECT 2)
- Use information effectively and creatively. (AASL/AECT 3)
- Practice ethical behavior in regard to information and information technology. (AASL/AECT 8)

Objectives

Small student groups research spiders and take notes in the prescribed way.

Directions

1. Copy the student worksheet on a transparency for use with an overhead projector. The library teacher explains the lesson using the overhead copy.
2. The library teacher explains that the island worksheet tree base is the main idea, and that the brief supporting facts are the tree leaves.
3. The science teacher assigns various spiders for small-group research. On the board, the teacher lists the main idea and supporting ideas. For example, students may find the eating habits, description, and other facts about selected spiders.
4. Small groups research and take notes on the island worksheets (being careful to not plagiarize).
5. Teachers monitor student work for understanding.

Learning Styles

Linguistic (reading and writing), mathematical (thinking logically), spatial (thinking visually), and interpersonal (working in groups).

Teaching Team

Library and science teachers.

Suggested Sources

Ethan, Eric. *Black Widow Spiders*. Milwaukee, WI: Gareth Stevens, 2004.
Gerholdt, James E. *Bird Eating Spiders*. Edina, MN: Abdo & Daughters, 1996.
Gerholdt, James E. *Jumping Spiders*. Edina, MN: Abdo & Daughters, 1996.
Gerholdt, James E. *Tarantula Spiders*. Edina, MN: Abdo & Daughters, 1996.
Holmes, Kevin J. *Spiders*. Mankato, MN: Capstone, 1998.
Murphy, Julie. *Wolf Spiders*. Edina, MN: Abdo & Daughters, 2004.
Solway, Andrew. *Deadly Spiders and Scorpions*. Chicago, IL: Heinemann, 2004.
Whitehouse, Patricia. *Trap-door Spiders*. Chicago, IL: Heinemann, 2004.

It's in the Bag!

There is a saying that says if you do well "It's in the bag!" The best book that everyone should read is in the bag! Give a book review about a really good book. Write a short paragraph that will grab everyone's attention, so that they will want to read the book too.

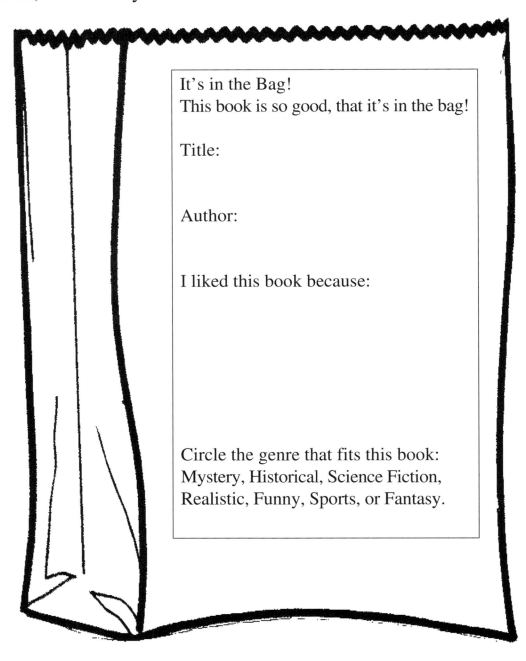

It's in the Bag!
This book is so good, that it's in the bag!

Title:

Author:

I liked this book because:

Circle the genre that fits this book:
Mystery, Historical, Science Fiction,
Realistic, Funny, Sports, or Fantasy.

It's in the Bag!

Standards

Students will

- Write in a variety of genres. (McREL 1)
- Use reading skills and strategies to understand a variety of familiar literary passages and text (e.g., fairy tales, folktales, fiction, nonfiction, fables, legends, poems, biographies). (McREL 9)
- Know the elements that compose a story. (e.g., character, plot, events, setting). (McREL 10)
- Appreciate and enjoy literature and other creative expressions of information. (AASL/AECT 5)

Objectives

Students tell about a fiction book and it's title, author, and genre.

Directions

1. The library and reading teachers talk about some good fiction books as they pull each one out of a paper sack. They give the title, author, a brief sketch, and genre.
2. On the worksheets, students write the title, author, and a brief description of their favorite book. Then they circle the genre.
3. After filling out their sheets, students display their work to spark others' interest to read. Students staple the worksheet sacks on a brown paper sack, then place the book on display with the sack. Sacks may also be displayed on a bulletin board.

Learning Styles

Linguistic (writing, reading) and intrapersonal (working alone).

Teaching Team

Library and reading teachers.

Suggested Sources

Avi. *The Secret School.* New York: Harcourt Brace, 2001.
Clements, Andrew. *The Jacket.* New York: Simon & Schuster, 2002.
DeFelice, Cynthia. *Death at Devil's Bridge.* New York: Farrar, Straus & Giroux, 2000.
Duffey, Betsy. *Cody Unplugged.* New York: Viking, 1999.
Jones, Elizabeth. *Watcher in Piney Woods.* New York: Pleasant Company, 2000.
Kehret, Peg. *Blizzard Disaster.* New York: Aladdin, 1998.
Levy, Elizabeth. *Vampire State Building.* New York: HarperCollins, 2002.
MacLachlan, Patrician. *Caleb's Story.* New York: HarperCollins, 2001.
Osborne, Mary Pope. *Tonight on the Titanic.* New York: Random House, 1999.
Scieszka, Jon. *It's All Greek to Me.* New York: Viking, 1999.
Wright, Betty Ben. *The Ghost in Room 11.* New York: Holiday House, 1998.

Sailing Internet Waters

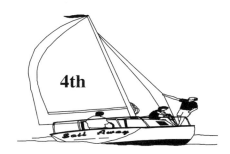

I. Do you know the Internet? Connect these words:

_____ 1. Computers connect world wide   A. Internet

_____ 2. Phone connection for Internet   C. URL

_____ 3. Internet software to browse Internet   B. Modem

_____ 4. Searches and connects to many special   F. Browser
       Internet sites

_____ 5. An Internet address (**U**niform **R**esource **L**ocater)   D. Homepage

_____ 6. Beginning or home page of an Internet site   E. Search Engine

II. Now sail the Internet:

1. Open up the browser software.

2. Find a search engine by typing it (http://www.yahooligans.com).

3. Find the search box and type the search word, Math.

4. Click on the blue words to link to a great site for your class! What is it?

URL (Internet address)   What's on this Internet site?

_____   _____

Sailing Internet Waters

Standards

Students will

- Use electronic media to gather information (e.g., Internet, videos). (McREL 4)
- Access information efficiently and effectively. (AASL/AECT 1)
- Evaluate information critically and competently. (AASL/AECT 2)
- Pursue information related to personal interests. (AASL/AECT 4)
- Use information effectively and creatively. (AASL/AECT 3)
- Recognize the importance of information to a democratic society. (AASL/AECT 8)

Objectives

Students discuss and complete a word match on Internet terms. Students search the Internet for educational sites.

Directions

1. The computer teacher lists and discusses these simple Internet terms: a) a *search engine* connects to many sites; b) a *modem* is a telephone connection; c) a *browser* is Internet software; d) a *homepage* is the beginning or first page of a site; e) the *Internet* connects computers; and f) a *URL* is an Internet address.
2. Teachers guide students as they match the Internet terms with the definitions on the worksheets.
3. Students use the Internet, after the computer or library teacher shows them the steps of opening up the browser and using a search engine to find a site.
4. Students use a child-safe search engine such as http://www.yahooligans.com. Following directions on the worksheets, student pairs search for a math site.
5. Students write the URL and a simple description of their educational site on their worksheets.
6. Students compare sites.

Learning Styles

Linguistic (writing), mathematical (using computers), and intrapersonal (working alone).

Teaching Team

Library and computer teachers.

Suggested Sources

Yahooligans is a safe search engine for kids: http://www.yahooligans.com

A Scared Rider

A scared rider from Sleepy Hollow.

1. Why did Ichabod Crane leave so quickly at the end of the story?

2. Who was the headless horseman according to old village stories? Who do you think was Ichabod's headless horseman?

3. Why did Brom Bones want Ichabod to leave?

4. The story of Ichabod Crane is a legend. What made it a legend?

A Scared Rider

Standards

Students will

- Write in a variety of genres. (McREL 1)
- Use reading skills and strategies to understand a variety of familiar literary passages and text (e.g., fairy tales, folktales, fiction, nonfiction, fables, legends, poems, biographies). (McREL 9)
- Know the elements that compose a story (e.g., character, plot, events, setting). (McREL 10)
- Appreciate and enjoy literature and other creative expressions of information. (AASL/AECT 5)

Objectives

Students listen to a legend as it is read to them and answer the story plot questions. They also make a doorknob holder.

Directions

1. The library teacher explains what makes a story a legend. For example the teacher may say that a legend takes place many years ago, is about a true character, and has been told many times. Then a shortened version of *The Legend of Sleepy Hollow* is told or read.
2. After the class hears the story, the reading teacher leads the class in completing the worksheet questions.
3. After writing their answers, students make a doorknob holder by cutting out the horseman square and the large circular doorknob hole.
4. If desired, students may color pumpkins and a night sky on the doorknob holder.

Learning Styles

Linguistic (reading, writing), spatial (coloring), intrapersonal (working alone), mathematical (thinking logically), and interpersonal (working in groups).

Teaching Team

Library and reading teachers.

Suggested Sources

Irving, Washington. *The Legend of Sleepy Hollow*. Thousand Oaks, CA: Monterey SoundWorks, 1999. [sound recording]

Jensen, Patsy. *The Legend of Sleepy Hollow*. Mahwah, NJ: Troll, 1994.

Standiford, Natalie. *The Headless Horseman*. New York: Random, 2003.

Tricky Words

Words can be tricky. Choose a word to fill in the blanks for the following sentences. It could be tricky! Some words could sound like the correct choice, but aren't the right ones.

Use the dictionary! Look up the tricky word choices. Choose the correct words to fit in each sentence!

1. Were you _____ to depart? Did you say that _____?
   aloud (or) *allowed*

2. Did you see how uncomplicated it was, _____? I only went _____ the dictionary twice.   *to* (or) *too*

3. The foremost point or _____ of the matter is that the _____ said it!   *principal* (or) *principle*

4. The message or _____ was sent by the newspaper _____.   *correspondents* (or) *correspondence*

5. Did you eat _____ before or after you went to the _____?
   desert (or) *dessert*

6. This may be an uncomplicated _____ that will _____ your spelling errors.   *lessen* (or) *lesson*

7. The hair cut will _____ you. You will like the _____.
   effect (or) *affect*

8. Were any of _____ questions right _____ for you, or were they difficult?   *there* (or) *their* (or) *they're*

From Joyce Keeling, *Lesson Plans for the Busy Librarian: A Standards Based Approach for the Elementary Library Media Center*, Volume 2. Westport, CT: Libraries Unlimited. © 2006.

Tricky Words

Standards

Students will

- Use a variety of resource materials to gather information for research topics (e.g., magazines, newspapers, dictionaries, schedules, journals, phone directories, globes, atlases, and almanacs). (McREL 7)
- Access information efficiently and effectively. (AASL/AECT 1)
- Evaluate information critically and competently. (AASL/AECT 2)
- Use information effectively and creatively. (AASL/AECT 3)

Objectives

Students use a dictionary to complete worksheet sentences.

Directions

1. The language arts and library teachers review the uses of dictionaries. Teachers then explain the directions on the student worksheet. Students find the meanings of word choices and decide which word best fits in the open sentence positions.
2. Teachers assist students working in pairs.
3. Once students complete their sheets, challenge them to write or illustrate sentences of other tricky word choices (could be extra credit).
4. Discuss and compare answers with the class.

Learning Styles

Mathematical (thinking logically), linguistic (writing), and interpersonal (working in a group)

Teaching Team

Language arts and library teachers.

Suggested Sources

Goldman, Jonathan L. (ed.). *Webster's New World Portable Large Print Dictionary*. New York: Prentice Hall, 1994.

World Book. *The World Book Student Dictionary*. Chicago, IL: World Book, Inc. 2001.

Rumpelstiltskin

This is the spinning wheel of the miller's daughter. In the 4 large areas of the wheel fully answer these questions by drawing or writing: (1) Why did the daughter try to spin gold? (2) What did the daughter give the little man at first? (3) What did she give him the second time? (4) How did it end?

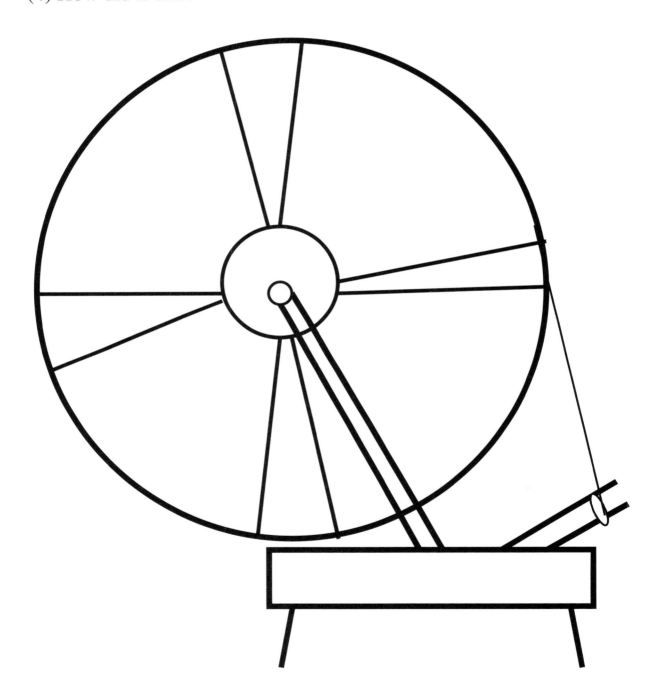

Rumpelstiltskin

Standards

Students will

- Write in a variety of genres. (McREL 1)
- Use reading skills and strategies to understand a variety of familiar literary passages and text (e.g., fairy tales, folktales, fiction, nonfiction, fables, legends, poems, bibliographies). (McREL 9)
- Know the elements that compose a story (e.g., character, plot, events, setting). (McREL 10)
- Appreciate and enjoy literature and other creative expressions of information. (AASL/AECT 5)

Objectives

Students listen to and discuss a fairy tale, then answer the worksheet questions.

Directions

1. The library and reading teachers read the *Rumpelstiltskin* fairy tale, while showing the illustrations.
2. Students answer questions as they hear the tale, fully writing their answers in the large areas of the worksheet spinning wheel. They may either draw or write the answers. Students write two or three complete sentences.
3. Teachers lead a discussion on plot, main character, and the worksheet answers.

Learning Styles

Linguistic (writing), spatial (drawing), and intrapersonal (working alone).

Teaching Team

Library and reading teachers.

Suggested Sources

Gavin, Marguerite. *Fifty Famous Fairy Tale Sound Recordings*. Askland, OR: Blackstone Audiobooks, 2000. [CD]

Martin, Annie-Claude. "Rumpelstiltskin." In *A Treasury of Fairy Tales*. Oxfordshire, England: Transedition Books, 1995.

Rowe, Gavin. "Rumpelstiltskin." In *Fairy Tales*. Newmarket, England: Brimax, 1996.

Stortz, Diane. *Rumpelstiltskin*. Ashland, OH: Landoll, 1994.

Zelinsky, Paul. *Rumpelstiltskin*. New York: Dutton, 1986.

Zelinsky, Paul. *Rumpelstiltskin*. Hightstown, NJ: American School Publishers, 1989. [Video]

Global View

1. On this globe, label the continents that you see.
2. In the boxes, list some of the countries in those continents.

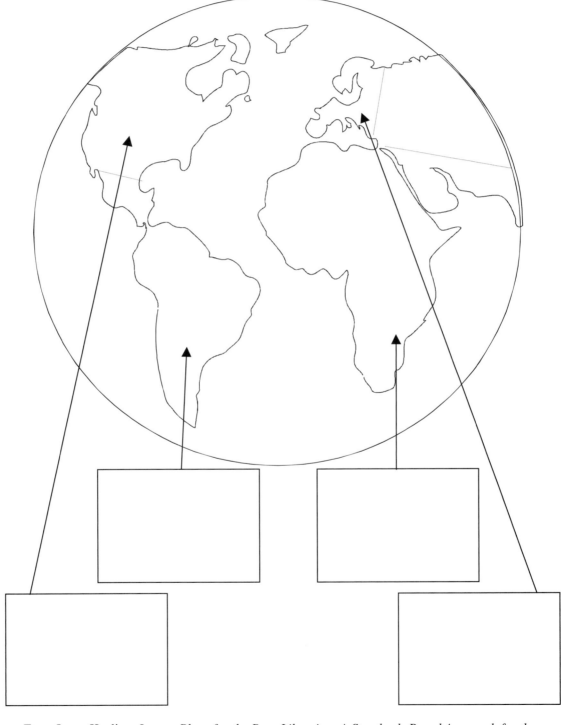

Global View

Standards

Students will

- Use electronic media to gather information (e.g., Internet, videos). (McREL 4)
- Use multiple representations of information (e.g., maps, charts, photos, diagrams, tables) to get information. (McREL 6)
- Use a variety of resource materials to gather information for research topics (e.g., magazines, newspapers, dictionaries, schedules, journals, phone directories, globes, atlases, and almanacs). (McREL 7)
- Access information efficiently and effectively. (AASL/AECT 1)
- Evaluate information critically and competently. (AASL/AECT 2)
- Use information effectively and creatively. (AASL/AECT 3)
- Strive for excellence in information seeking and knowledge generation. (AASL/AECT 6)
- Recognize the importance of information to a democratic society. (AASL/AECT 7)

Objectives

Students use an atlas to label four continents and then name some of the countries on the continents. Students use an online source to verify their answers.

Directions

1. Student pairs or small groups use atlases to locate and label the continents of North America, South America, Africa, and Europe on their worksheet globes.
2. Student pairs or small groups then list some of the countries on the continents after the social studies teacher explains how many countries are to be listed.
3. After completing their sheets, students may look on an online site to check their papers for accuracy and check their own understanding.

Learning Styles

Linguistic (writing), spatial (reading maps), mathematical (using computers), and interpersonal (working in groups).

Teaching Team

Library and social studies teachers.

Suggested Sources

Rand McNally. *Goode's World Atlas*. Skookie, IL: Rand McNally, 1999.
Rand McNally. *Rand McNally Premier World Atlas*. Skookie, IL: Rand McNally, 1997.
World Book. *World Book Atlas*. Chicago, IL: World Book, 2004.
Infoplease Web site: http://www.infoplease.com/atlas

The Magic Lamp

Rub the magic lamp! Make the plot, setting and characters appear!

1. Who were the main characters: _____

    _____

2. What was the main plot? _____

    _____

3. Where was the setting? _____

    _____

4. If you could change the story, how would it be?_____

    _____

5. If you could rub the magic lamp, for what would you ask? _____

    _____

The Magic Lamp

Standards

Students will

- Write in a variety of genres. (McREL 1)
- Use reading skills and strategies to understand a variety of familiar literary passages and text (e.g., fairy tales, folktales, fiction, nonfiction, fables, legends, poems, biographies). (McREL 9)
- Know the elements that compose a story. (McREL 10)
- Appreciate and enjoy literature and other creative expressions of information. (AASL/AECT 5)
- Recognize the importance of information to a democratic society. (AASL/AECT 7)
- Practice ethical behavior in regard to information and information technology. (AASL/AECT 8)

Objectives

Students hear an Aladdin story and then answer s questions on its plot, character, setting, and a possible story change.

Directions

1. The library teacher reads or tells a story about Aladdin that includes a magic lamp.
2. Students explain why the story is considered a fantasy. Then students answer their worksheet questions on the plot, main characters, setting, and a possible story change. The teachers check for understanding as they help students.
3. After completing the worksheets, the class compares answers.
4. Finally, students write down a wish they have for a magic lamp.

Learning Styles

Linguistic (writing), mathematical (thinking logically), spatial (imagining), and intrapersonal (working alone).

Teaching Team

Library and reading teachers.

Suggested Sources

Horowit, Jordan. *Aladdin and the Magic Lamp*. New York: Scholastic, 1993.
Kerven, Rosalind. *Aladdin*. New York: Dorling Kindersley, 2000.
Martin, Annie-Claudie. *A Treasury of Fairy Tales*. Spain: Transedition Books, 1995.
Rowe, Gavin. *Fairy Tales*. New Market, England: Brimax, 1996.
Tenggren, Gustaf. *Tenggren's Golden Tales From the Arabian Nights*. New York: Golden Books, 2003.
Trussell, Cullen Alan. *Aladdin and the Magic Lamp*. Carlsbad, CA: Dominie Press, 2000.

Piñata Time!

Color the two horses in bright colors. Tape the horses together leaving only a top opening. Give it as a gift! Write 2–3 small positive notes about the person who will get this gift. Put the notes in the horses. Tape the horses shut. Attach colorful ribbons. It's a miniature piñata!

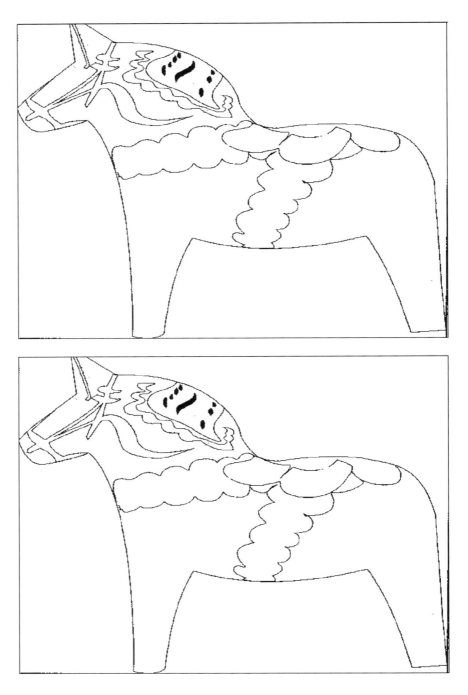

Piñata Time!

Standards

Students will

- Use reading skills and strategies to understand a variety of familiar literary passages and text (e.g., fairy tales, folktales, fiction, nonfiction, fables, legends, poems, biographies). (McREL 9)
- Recognize the importance of information to a democratic society. (AASL/AECT 7)

Objectives

Students hear about a Mexican Christmas holiday and create a miniature piñata.

Directions

1. The social studies teacher reads and discusses how people of Mexican or Hispanic heritage celebrate Christmas. The library teacher reads either a book on Los Pasados or something else on Mexican Christmas holiday traditions. A discussion follows.
2. Since piñatas are used with many Mexican celebrations, including Christmas, students make a miniature piñata. They may give the miniature piñatas as a gift.
3. The art teacher directs the activity. Students color the two worksheet horses, then tape the two horses together, leaving a small opening at the top.
4. Students write 2 or 3 small positive notes about a person to whom their piñata will be given. They insert their note into their piñata.
5. Colorful ribbons are added to the horses. Then the piñatas are given away.

Learning Styles

Spatial (creating, coloring) and intrapersonal (working alone).

Teaching Team

Social studies, art, and library teachers.

Suggested Sources

dePaola, Tomie. *The Night of Las Posadas.* New York: Putman, 1999.

Dillon, Susan. *The Scholastic Big Book of Holidays Around the Year.* New York: Scholastic, 2003.

Hoyt-Goldsmith, Diane. *Las Posadas: A Hispanic Christmas.* New York: Holiday House, 1999.

Kalman, Bobbie. *We Celebrate Christmas.* New York: Crabtree, 1985.

Kelley, Emily. *Christmas Around the World.* Minneapolis, MN: Carolrhoda, 2003.

Kindersley, Anabel. *Celebrations Around the World.* New York: Dorling Kindersley, 1997.

Sadler, Judy Ann. *Christmas Crafts from Around the World.* New York: Kids Can Press, 2003.

Solar System Calendar

Make a Solar System Calendar!

1. Choose a planet or another solar system subject. Write the solar system name at the top. Write two facts.

2. Add a colorful picture.

3. Add the calendar month, days, and year.

4. Staple your calendar with other copies to make a full solar system calender

Label the planet or subject ⟹

_____

Create colorful picture ⟹

Write 2 facts ⟹

_____

_____

Write month/year ⟹

Sun.	Mon.	Tue.	Wed.	Thurs.	Fri.	Sat.

From Joyce Keeling, *Lesson Plans for the Busy Librarian: A Standards Based Approach for the Elementary Library Media Center*, Volume 2. Westport, CT: Libraries Unlimited. © 2006.

Solar System Calendar

Standards

Students will

- Use electronic media to gather information (e.g., Internet, videos). (McREL 4)
- Use reading skills and strategies to understand a variety of familiar literary passages and text (e.g., fairy tales, folktales, fiction, nonfiction, fables, legends, poems, biographies). (McREL 9)
- Access information efficiently and effectively. (AASL/AECT 1)
- Evaluate information critically and competently. (AASL/AECT 2)
- Use information effectively and creatively. (AASL/AECT 3)

Objectives

Students create a solar system class calendar by illustrating and writing two facts about either a planet, the moon, the sun, or comets.

Directions

1. Students create a solar system class calendar, perhaps for the new year. This may take two library periods.
2. The science teacher assigns to a small group or pair of students one of comets, sun, moon, or a planet. The teacher suggests two facts to be found. An example for planets: students may write the distance from the sun and another fact
3. The library teacher guides student research.
4. Students colorfully illustrate their subject at the top of their pages and label it.
5. In math and/or in another library class, students are assigned a month and use an almanac to fill in the calendar dates, months, and year.
6. Student pages are copied and stapled for student desk calendars.

Learning Styles

Linguistic (reading, writing), spatial (coloring), mathematical (making calendars), interpersonal (working with others), and intrapersonal (coloring).

Teaching Team

Library and science teachers.

Suggested Sources

Brimner, Larry Dane. *Pluto.* Chicago, IL: Children's Press, 1991.
Goldstein, Margaret. *Saturn.* Minneapolis, MN: Lerner, 2004.
Meachem, Dana. *Venus.* Minneapolis, MN: Compass Books, 2002.
Riley, Peter. *Our Solar System.* Wesport, CT: Joshua Morris Publishing, 1996.
World Almanac. *World Almanac and Book of Facts.* Chicago, IL: World Almanac, 2005.
Planet sites on the Internet:
http://www.dustbunny.com/afk/planets
http://www.nineplanets.org

Inventors, Inventing

Be an inventor! Find a biography book of an inventor. Write on the following note pad, like the inventor might have done when he/she was inventing. Write the inventor's name at the top. Then write (1) What and when one thing was invented, and (2) Write 3–5 facts about the inventor's life. (3) Finally draw a sketch of the invention such as he/she would have made.

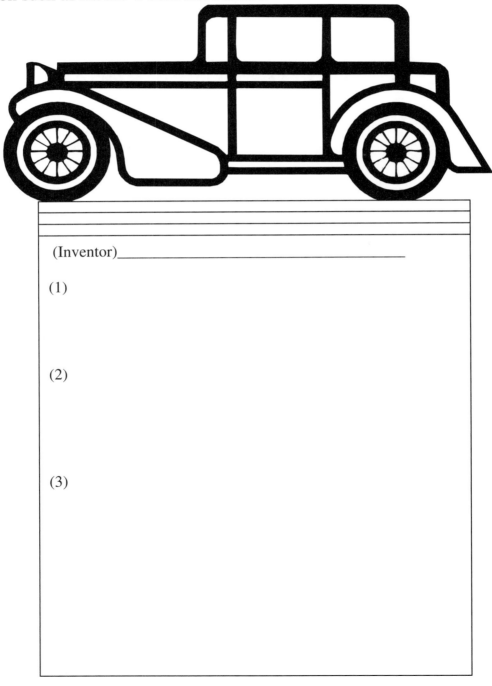

(Inventor)_____

(1)

(2)

(3)

Inventors, Inventing

Standards

Students will:

- Write in a variety of genres. (McREL 1)
- Use multiple representations of information (e.g., maps, charts, photos, diagrams, tables) to get information. (McREL 6)
- Use reading skills and strategies to understand a variety of familiar literary passages and text (e.g., fairy tales, folktales, fiction, nonfiction, fables, legends, poems, biographies). (McREL 9)
- Access information efficiently and effectively. (AASL/AECT 1)
- Evaluate information critically and competently. (AASL/AECT 2)
- Use information effectively and creatively. (AASL/AECT 3)
- Pursue information related to personal interests. (AASL/AECT 4)

Objectives

Students research and write about an inventor and sketch the invention.

Directions

1. The social studies teacher has students list some inventors on the board.
2. The library teacher shows students how to find biography books on inventors.
3. Small groups research an inventor and invention. Each student writes what was invented, when it was invented, and three facts about the inventor's life on the worksheet notepad.
4. Students find a sketch or picture of the invention, and draw a simple sketch of it, such as the inventor might have drawn.
5. Students present their facts and show their sketch to the class.

Learning Styles

Linguistic (writing, reading), spatial (drawing), mathematical (thinking logically), interpersonal (working in groups), and intrapersonal (working alone).

Teaching Team

Social studies and library teachers.

Suggested Sources

Adler, David. *Benjamin Franklin*. New York: Holiday House, 1990.
Bagley, Katie. *Eli Whitney: American Inventor*. Mankato, MN: Bridgestone, 2003.
Ford, Carin T. *Henry Ford*. Berkeley Heights, NJ: Enslow, 2003.
Joseph, Paul. *Alexander Graham Bell*. Edina, MN: Abdo and Daughters, 1997.
Mara, Wil. *Thomas Alva Edison*. Chicago, IL: Children's Press, 2004.
Schaefer, Lola. *The Wright Brothers*. Mankato, MN: Pebble Books, 2000.

Soaring with Magazines

Magazines have fiction and nonfiction articles on jets and other interesting things. Find a magazine that has a nonfiction article.

Skim the nonfiction magazine article.

1. List some facts from that article:

_____

_____

_____

2. Who is the author of the article? _____

3. What is the article title? _____

4. What is the title of the magazine? _____

5. What is the date of the magazine _____

6. What are the page numbers of your article?_____

7. Now, write a magazine bibliography using the following example. Keeling, Adam. "Flying the Skies." *Space World.* 15 June 2006: 13–15.

_____

_____

Did you happen to find a joke in a magazine? Write it down:

_____

_____

Soaring with Magazines

Standards

Students will

- Write in a variety of genres. (McREL 1)
- Use a variety of resource materials to gather information for research topics (e.g., magazines, newspapers, dictionaries, schedules, journals, phone directories, globes, atlases, and almanacs). (McREL 7)
- Access information efficiently and effectively. (AASL/AECT 1)
- Evaluate information critically and competently. (AASL/AECT 2)
- Use information effectively and creatively. (AASL/AECT 3)
- Pursue information related to personal interests. (AASL/AECT 4)
- Practice ethical behavior in regard to information and information technology. (AASL/AECT 8)

Objectives

Students locate a nonfiction magazine article, write two or three facts, and then write the bibliography.

Directions

1. The library teacher points out various magazines that are interesting to fourth graders, pointing out each magazine's title and date. The teacher shows examples of fiction and non-fiction articles.

2. Student pairs select a nonfiction magazine article and write the magazine title, date, article title, article author, page, and two or three facts from that article. Students are reminded not to plagiarize. Teachers assist.

3. The language arts teacher explains bibliography. The teacher tells students that worksheet numbers two through six are listed in the exact order that the bibliography description is written, so students can simply copy down the facts in order of the questions to complete the bibliography item for their article. Teachers help.

Learning Styles

Linguistic (reading and writing) and intrapersonal (working in pairs).

Teaching Team

Language arts and library teachers.

Suggested Sources

Cobblestone, *Kids Discover*, *Sports Illustrated for Kids*, and *Zoobooks* magazines.

Great Casey!

Casey was a great player. Make a baseball card of the great Casey. (1) Put his name on the card. (2) Put some information about him on the back. (3) On the front, draw a picture of Casey or use the following figure. (4) Color the card.

Great Casey!

Standards

Students will

- Write in a variety of genres. (McREL 1)
- Use reading skills and strategies to understand a variety of familiar literary passages and text (e.g., fairy tales, folktales, fiction, nonfiction, fables, legends, poems, biographies). (McREL 9)
- Know the elements that compose a story (e.g., character, plot, events, setting). (McREL 10)
- Appreciate and enjoy literature and other creative expressions of information. (AASL/AECT 5)

Objectives

Students hear and discuss the poem/ballad of "Casey at the Bat." Students learn about baseball cards and finally create a Casey baseball card.

Directions

1. Copy the student worksheet on cardstock or sturdy paper.
2. The library teacher reads "Casey at the Bat" while showing illustrations.
3. The reading teacher discusses plot, setting, and character.
4. The library teacher shows students what a baseball card looks like either from a book or online source. After explaining and giving examples of baseball players' batting average statistics, the class will create a fictional statistical batting average for Casey.
5. Students create Casey baseball cards. On the front, they draw and color a picture of Casey or use the given figure. They also write "Casey" in bold letters on front.
6. On the back of the cards, students write one to two biographical sentences on Casey as learned from "Casey at the Bat," and then write the class-created statistics.
7. Students cut out the baseball cards.

Learning Styles

Linguistic (writing), spatial (creating), interpersonal (working with others), and intrapersonal (working alone).

Teaching Team

Library and reading teachers.

Suggested Sources

Owens, Tom. *Collecting Baseball Cards*. New York: Millbrook Press, 2001.

Thayer, Ernest Laurence. *Casey at the Bat: A Ballad of the Republic Sung in the Year 1888*. New York: Scholastic, 2001.

Web site of the Major League Baseball Association at http://www.mlb.com

Treasures of Information

The almanac has treasures of facts on almost everything. Use an almanac. Go on a treasure hunt to find one fact on each of the following subjects:

1. Sports: _____

_____

2. Nation or Country: _____

_____

3. Astronomy: _____

_____

4. Disasters: _____

_____

5. Computers: _____

_____

Did you find a fact on every subject? You won the gold!

Treasures of Information

Standards

Students will

- Write in a variety of genres. (McREL 1)
- Use electronic media to gather information (e.g., Internet, videos). (McREL 4)
- Use a variety of resource materials to gather information for research topics (e.g., newspapers, dictionaries, schedules, journals, phone directories, globes, atlases, and almanacs). (McREL 7)
- Access information efficiently and effectively. (AASL/AECT 1)
- Evaluate information critically and competently. (AASL/AECT 2)
- Use information effectively and creatively. (AASL/AECT 3)
- Pursue information related to personal interests. (AASL/AECT 4)
- Strive for excellence in information seeking and knowledge generation. (AASL/AECT 6)
- Practice ethical behavior in regard to information and information technology. (AASL/AECT 8)
- Participate effectively in groups to pursue and generate information. (AASL/AECT 9)

Objectives

Students use an almanac to locate and write facts.

Directions

1. The library teacher explains that an almanac has facts on almost everything, and shows students how to locate facts in almanacs.
2. The language arts teacher divides students into small teams.
3. The teams find facts on the worksheet subjects and write them down. Students may locate the first four subjects in the print format and find the final subject online. Students are reminded to avoid plagiarism.
4. Time how long it takes the teams to finish.
5. Teams read some of their answers to the class.

Learning Styles

Mathematical (using computers), linguistic (writing, reading, trivia), and interpersonal (working in groups).

Teaching Team

Language arts and library teachers.

Suggested Sources

McGeveran, William Jr.soloar system
The World Almanac and Book of Facts 2004. New York: World Almanac, 2004.

Information Please Almanac Internet site: http://www.infoplease.com/almanac

Leaping Leprechauns!

A limerick is a five-line poem with lines 1, 2, and 5 rhyming, and lines 3 and 4 rhyming. Limericks are funny. Read the following limerick example. Then, write your own limerick about a leprechaun.

A leaping leprechaun danced in the rain,

Which provided quite a pain,

When he landed wrong on his tippy toes.

For he fell down and broke his great nose,

And had to carefully jig-jog back down the street of main!

_____

_____

_____

_____

_____

Leaping Leprechauns!

Standards

Students will

- Write in a variety of genres. (McREL 1)
- Use reading skills and strategies to understand a variety of familiar literary passages and text (e.g., fairy tales, folktales, fiction, nonfiction, fables, legends, poems, biographies). (McREL 9)
- Appreciate and enjoy literature and other creative expressions of information. (AASL/AECT 5)
- Strive for excellence in information and knowledge generation. (AASL/AECT 6)
- Recognize the importance of information to a democratic society. (AASL/AECT 7)

Objectives

Students create and write a limerick about a leprechaun for St. Patrick's Day.

Directions

1. The library teacher reads a St. Patrick's story.
2. The language arts teacher explains that limericks are sometimes associated with the Irish, so students create a limerick about a leprechaun for St. Patrick's Day. The teacher reads how limericks are constructed from the student worksheet.
3. The language arts and library teachers give examples of limericks.
4. Students write their limericks on their worksheets. If desired, they may type their limerick.
5. Once limericks are completed, students color the leprechaun and attach it to their individual poems.

Learning Styles

Linguistic (writing, reading), spatial (coloring), musical (rhyming), and intrapersonal (working alone).

Teaching Team

Computer, language arts, and library teachers.

Suggested Sources

Ciardi, John. *The Hopeful Trout and Other Limericks*. New York: Houghton Mifflin, 1989.
Freeman, Dorothy Rhodes. *St. Patrick's Day*. New York: Enslow, 1992.
Kissel, Joyce. *St. Patrick's Day*. New York: Carolrhoda, 1982.
Livingston, Myra Cohn. *Limericks*. New York: M.K. McElderry, 1991.
Internet Limerick page: http://www.schoollink.org/csd/pages/engl/limerick.html [limericks]

Tricky Coyote's Circle

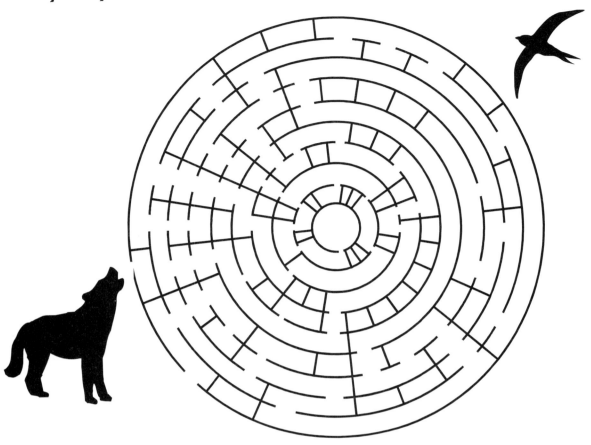

Tricky Coyote (or another Coyote) was at the center of some Native American/ Indian stories. His stories led into a circle of confusion, which made it hard for other creatures or even Coyote to escape. Read about Tricky Coyote or another Native American Coyote.

1. The setting is _____

2. Who did Coyote trick (or who tried to trick Coyote)? _____
   Write that name in the middle of the maze also.

3. What happened to Coyote in the end? _____

   _____

   _____

4. Now complete the Coyote's maze.

From Joyce Keeling, *Lesson Plans for the Busy Librarian: A Standards Based Approach for the Elementary Library Media Center*, Volume 2. Westport, CT: Libraries Unlimited. © 2006.

Tricky Coyote's Circle

Standards

Students will

- Use reading skills and strategies to understand a variety of familiar literary passages and text (e.g., fairy tales, folktales, fiction, nonfiction, fables, legends, poems, biographies). (McREL 9)
- Know the elements that compose a story (e.g., character, plot, events, setting). (McREL 10)
- Appreciate and enjoy literature and other creative expressions of information. (AASL/AECT 5)
- Participate effectively in groups to pursue and generate information. (AASL/AECT 9)

Objectives

Students hear, discuss, and write the plots, character, and setting of a Native American/Indian coyote tale.

Directions

1. The reading teacher reads or tells a Tricky Coyote or other Native American/Indian coyote tale.
2. Following the story, the library teacher asks students to explain the beginning, middle, and the ending plots, as well as setting and characters.
3. Teachers assist students in answering the worksheet questions.
4. Students complete the maze.

Learning Styles

Linguistic (writing), mathematical (thinking logical), spatial (doing puzzles), interpersonal (discussing), and intrapersonal (working alone).

Teaching Team

Library and reading teachers.

Suggested Sources

Bierhorst, John. *Doctor Coyote*. New York: Macmillan, 1987.
Mayo, Gretchen Will. *Meet Tricky Coyote!* New York: Walker and Company, 1993.
Mayo, Gretchen Will. *That Tricky Coyote! (Native American Trickster Tales)*. New York: Walker and Company, 1993.
McDermott, Gerald. *Coyote*. New York: Harcourt Brace & Co., 1994.

Rain Forest

Create a rain forest locker poster. Draw and color trees on the blank poster. Color the snake, baboon, parrot, toucan, tiger, and tree frog to add them.

Rain Forest

From Joyce Keeling, *Lesson Plans for the Busy Librarian: A Standards Based Approach for the Elementary Library Media Center*, Volume 2. Westport, CT: Libraries Unlimited. © 2006.

Rain Forest

Standards

Students will

- Write in a variety of genres. (McREL 1)
- Use electronic media to gather information (e.g., Internet, videos). (McREL 4)
- Use reading skills and strategies to understand a variety of familiar literary passages, forms, and text (e.g., fairy tales, folktales, fiction, nonfiction, fables, legends, poems, biographies). (McREL 9)
- Access information efficiently and effectively. (AASL/AECT 1)
- Evaluate information critically and competently. (AASL/AECT 2)
- Use information effectively and creatively. (AASL/AECT 3)

Objectives

Students write 3–5 sentences on the Bengal tiger, gorilla, toucan, green snake, tree frog, and parrot. They design a rain forest poster with those rain forest animals.

Directions

1. This lesson takes two class sessions.
2. Students, with the science teacher, list rain forest animals on the board. Then they search for a picture of a rain forest, and find facts and pictures of the Bengal tiger, gorilla, toucan, green snake, parrot, and tree frog.
3. The library teacher assists students in their research.
4. After finding pictures, students draw a rain forest with green trees of various sizes on their worksheet locker posters. They color it and add the colored animals.
5. With the science teacher, students write 3–5 sentences about each animal on a separate paper to be attached to bottom of the posters. Students may work in groups to collect facts.
6. The rain forest posters may be hung on student lockers.

Learning Styles

Linguistic (writing, reading), spatial (coloring), and interpersonal (working alone).

Teaching Team

Library and science teachers.

Suggested Sources

Burnie, David. *The Kingfisher Illustrated Animal Encyclopedia.* New York: Kingfisher, 2000.
Cowley, Joy. *Red-Eyed Tree Frog.* New York: Scholastic, 1999.
Gerholdt, James E. *Amazon Parrots.* Edina, MN: Abdo & Daughters, 1997.
Stone, Lynn M. *Gorillas.* Vero Beach, FL: Rourke, 1990.
Swartz, David M. *Green Snake.* Milwaukee, WI: Gareth Stevens, 2001.
Theodore, Rod. *Bengal Tiger.* Chicago, IL: Heinemann Library, 2001.
Enchanted Learning site offers rain forest facts: http://www.enchantedlearning.com/subjects/rainforest/animals

Sports Are Fun!

Think of a sport. Write a list of action words about your sport! Make all the words have the same ending. You now have created a list poem! Add a title!

Sports Are Fun!

Standards

Students will

- Write in a variety of genres. (McREL 1)
- Use the library catalog. (McREL 3)
- Use strategies to gather information (e.g., notes). (McREL 8)
- Use reading skills and strategies to understand a variety of familiar literary passages and text (e.g., fairy tales, folktales, fiction, nonfiction, fables, legends, poems, biographies). (McREL 9)
- Access information efficiently and effectively. (AASL/AECT 1)
- Evaluate information critically and competently. (AASL/AECT 2)
- Use information effectively and creatively. (AASL/AECT 3)
- Pursue information related to personal interests. (AASL/AECT 4)

Objectives

Students research a sport and create a list poem.

Directions

1. A teacher demonstrates how to create a list poem. The word *swimming* is written on the board, and then action words that all have the same ending are listed, such as *diving, splashing, jumping, floating, treading, plunging,* or *racing.*
2. Students write a sport on the top of their paper for a list poem title.
3. Students browse sports sources for action word ideas as the library teacher assists.
4. Teachers help students list action words for their sport, thus creating a list poem.

Learning Styles

Linguistic (writing, reading), musical (rhyming), and intrapersonal (working alone).

Teaching Team

Library and physical education teachers.

Suggested Sources

Buckley, James Jr. *Play Ball!* New York: Dorling Kindersley, 2002.
Doeden, Matt. *Skateboarding.* Minneapolis, MN, 2005.
Gibbons, Gail. *My Soccer Book.* New York: HarperCollins, 2000.
Joseph, Paul. *Basketball.* Edina, MN: Abdo & Daughters, 1996.
Joseph, Paul. *Gymnastics.* Edina, MN: Abdo & Daughters, 1996.
Kalman, Bobbie. *Vollyball in Action.* New York: Crabtree, 2000.
Kalman, Bobbie. *Football in Action.* New York: Crabtree, 2000.
Martin, John. *In-Line Skating.* Minneapolis, MN: Capstone, 1994.
Noble, Jim. *Swimming.* New York: Bookwright, 1991.

Chapter 6

Fifth Grade Lesson Plans

A solid, professionally based library lesson plan is built around developmental needs of students at their grade level, the Kendall and Marzano or McREL: National Education Language Arts Standards and Benchmarks, the AASL (American Association of School Libraries), and the AECT (Association for Educational Communications and Technology) Information Literacy Standards, and around the various learning styles of students as found in Gardner's Multiple Intelligences framework. (The selected AASL/AECT standards and Gardner's Multiple Intelligences are fully described in the introduction.) All of the following lessons are built around these standards, benchmarks, and skills in order to ensure that all students appreciate different forms of literature and are competent users of information, and so become information literate.

Each lesson plan includes student objectives, team teaching suggestions, and suggested sources. Furthermore, each lesson is designed to last approximately twenty minutes. All lessons have been field-tested. The lessons provide individual or small-group worksheet work and are designed to make library learning enjoyable, to be easily accomplished in a librarian's or library teacher's busy schedule, and to be grounded in solid standards and benchmarks. Each lesson has a reference to the following McREL standards and benchmarks, as well as a reference to the AASL/AECT standards.

Fifth Grade Library Standards and Language Arts Benchmarks (McCREL)

Reprinted by permission of McREL

Fifth grade students will be able to:

Use the general skills and strategies of the writing process. (Standard 1)

1. Write in a variety of forms of genre. (Standard 1, Benchmark 7, under grades K-2)

Gather and use information for research purposes. (Standard 4)

2. Use encyclopedias to gather information. (Standard 4, Benchmark 2)
3. Use library catalog (Standard 4, Benchmark 2, under grades 6–8)
4. Use electronic media to gather information (e.g., Internet, videos). (Standard 4, Benchmark 4)
5. Use key words, guide words, alphabetical and numerical order, indexes, cross references, and letters on volumes to find information for research topics. (Standard 4, Benchmarks 5)
6. Use a variety of resources materials to gather information for research topics (e.g., magazines, newspapers, dictionaries, schedules, journals, phone, directories, globes, atlases, and almanacs). (Standard 4, Benchmark 4, under grades 6–8)

Use reading skills and strategies to understand and interpret a variety of literary texts. (Standard 6)

7. Use reading skills and strategies to understand a variety of familiar literary passages and text (e.g., fairy tales, folktales, fiction, nonfiction, fables, legends, poems, biographies). (Standard 6, Benchmark 1)
8. Know the elements that compose a story (e.g., character, plot, events, setting). (Standard 6, Benchmark 2, under Pre-K)

Use reading skills and strategies to understand and interpret a variety of informational texts. (Standard 7)

9. Use the various parts of a book. (Standard 7, Benchmark 4)

Talking About Books!

Talking about books:

✓ Show enthusiasm

✓ Show the book

✓ Tell title & author

✓ Tell exciting parts

✓ *Never* tell the end

✓ Talk 2-3 minutes

Talk about a book you liked!

1. First, you'll need to find a book you like. Then read the entire book! Now, get ready to tell about it.

2. Follow the rules in the box above. Color the checkmarks after you are ready to follow that booktalking rule.

3. Now give your booktalk. Remember that the purpose of a booktalk is to convince others to read your book.

From Joyce Keeling, *Lesson Plans for the Busy Librarian: A Standards Based Approach for the Elementary Library Media Center*, Volume 2. Westport, CT: Libraries Unlimited. © 2006.

Talking About Books!

Standards

Students will

- Use reading skills and strategies to understand a variety of familiar literary passages and text (e.g. fairy tales, folktales, fiction, nonfiction, fables, legends, poems, biographies). (McREL 7)
- Appreciate and enjoy literature and other creative expressions of information. (AASL/AECT 5)

Objectives

Students learn how to give a book talk. Students book talk a book after choosing one.

Directions

1. This lesson takes more than one class period.
2. The library and reading teachers book talk some exciting books for the students.
3. Teachers go over the book talking rules on the student worksheet.
4. Students choose a book to read for their own book talks. They are told the due date when their book must be read and their book talk given to the class (4–6 weeks).
5. Students either book talk in their library or in their reading classroom.

Learning Styles

Linguistic (reading) and intrapersonal (working alone)

Teaching Team

Library and reading teachers

Suggested Sources

Coville, Bruce. *The Monsters of Morely Manor*. New York: Harcourt 2001
Crilley, Mark. *Akiko on the Planet Smoo*. NY: Hyperion, 2000.
Denenberg, Barry. *Early Sunday Morning: The Pearl Harbor Diary of Amber Bellows*.
 New York: Scholastic, 2001.
Gutman, Dan. *The Million Dollar Kick*. NY: Hyperion, 2001.
Hobbs, Will. *Jason's Gold*. New York: Morrow Junior, 1999.
Mundis, Heather. *My Chimp Friday*. New York: Simon & Schuster, 2002.
Naylor, Phyllis Reynolds. *The Boy's Return*. New York: Delacorte Press, 2001.
Roberts, Willo Davis. *Hostage*. New York: Atheneum, 2000.
Snicket, Lemony. *The Reptile Room*. New York: HarperCollins, 1999.

Entry—The Entrance

A dictionary entry opens up doorways to lots of information about a word. A dictionary entry can give parts of speech (such as noun, verb, adjective, adverb), cross-references, word forms (plurals), pronunciation, and definition. Use the following entries to answer the questions.

Break (brak) *v* - 1. To force apart. 2. Stop.   Broke, Broken, Breaking

Broke - *See* Break.

Explore (ek splawr) *v* - 1. To travel. 2. Investigation.   Exploration *n*.

Latitude (lat e tud) *n* - 1. Distance from the equator measured by going across parallel east to west. 2. Freedom of choice.   Latitudes *n*

Launch (lawnch) *v* - 1. Send into space or afloat. 2. To begin.   Launching *n*

Monotonous (ma not a nes) *adj* - Boring because it is the same.

1. What part of speech is *Monotonous*? Write a *Monotonous* thought.

2. What is the cross-reference for *Broke*? Why is it a cross-reference?

3. Is there a definition of *Latitude* that is new to you? Why?

4. What are the two parts of speech for *Explore*?

5. Use one of the forms of the word *Break* in a short sentence.

6. Illustrate the pronunciation of the word *Launch*.

From Joyce Keeling, *Lesson Plans for the Busy Librarian: A Standards Based Approach for the Elementary Library Media Center*, Volume 2. Westport, CT: Libraries Unlimited. © 2006.

Entry—The Entrance

Standards

Students will

- Write in a variety of forms of genre. (McREL 1)
- Use key words, guidewords, alphabetical and numerical order, indexes, crossreferences, and letters on volumes to find information for research topics. (McREL 5)
- Use a variety of resource materials to gather information for research topics (e.g. magazines, newspapers, dictionaries, schedules, journals, phone directories, globes, atlases, and almanacs). (McREL 6)
- Use information effectively and creatively. (AASL/AECT 3)
- Strive for excellence in information seeking and knowledge generation. (AASL/AECT 6)
- Participate effectively in groups to purse and generate information. (AASL/AECT 9)

Objectives

Students review the use of a dictionary, and then answer their worksheet questions using the dictionary entries provided.

Directions

1. The library teacher reviews how to use a dictionary, including cross-reference use.
2. The language arts teacher asks students to explain what information is found in a dictionary, such as parts of speech and word plurals. Students are also encouraged to give word definitions, word spellings, and pronunciations.
3. Students read the dictionary entries found on their worksheets and answer the questions. Students may work in small groups.
4. When work is completed, students share their answers.

Learning Styles

Mathematical (thinking logically), linguistic (reading, writing), interpersonal (working in groups), and intrapersonal (working alone)

Teaching Team

Language arts and library teachers

Suggested Sources

Goldman, Jonathan L., Ed. *Webster's New World Portable Large Print Dictionary*. New York: Prentice Hall, 1994.

World Book. *The Student World Book Student Dictionary*. Chicago, Ill.: World Book, Inc. 2001.

Davy Crockett

Davy Crockett ran for the state legislature. Make a poster to promote him as the best person for the legislature. Find information about him from his biography or from his tall tales, and then write two- or three-word phrases on Davy Crockett's poster to promote him as the best candidate.

Davy Crockett for Office!

Davy Crockett

Standards

Students will

- Write in a variety of forms of genre. (McREL 1)
- Use reading skills and strategies to understand a variety of familiar literary passages and text (e.g. fairy tales, folktales, fiction, nonfiction, fables, legends, poems, biographies). (McREL 7)
- Evaluate information critically and competently. (AASL/AECT 2)
- Use information effectively and creatively. (AASL/AECT 3)
- Recognize the importance of information to a democratic society. (AASL/AECT 7)

Objectives

Students listen to both a biography and tall tale of Davy Crockett, and compare the two. They will create a Davy Crockett campaign poster.

Directions

1. On the board, teachers create a Venn diagram by drawing two interlocking circles to compare a tall tale and a biography of Davy Crockett. The library teacher reads a portion of a Davy Crockett tall tale and asks students what is factual and what is far-fetched.
2. The social studies teacher reads some of Davy Crockett's biography. Students will then list facts from this source in the right Venn diagram. Comparisons should be made between the biography and the tall tale in the middle Venn circular diagram.
3. Students will create Davy Crockett campaign posters of his life achievements. Students will use the diagram or what they heard to write real or outlandish slogans reflecting Davy Crockett's life. Slogans will be written on posters at various angles in bright colors.
4. Students should color worksheet posters before having them displayed.

Learning Styles

Linguistic (writing), Spatial (creating, imagining), and Intrapersonal (working alone)

Teaching Team

Library and social studies teachers

Suggested Sources

Alphin, Elaine Marie. *Davy Crockett*. New York: Barnes & Noble, 2002.

"Crockett, Davy." *World Book Encyclopedia*. Chicago, ILL: World Book, 2005.

Feeney, Kathy. *Davy Crockett: A Photo-Illustrated Biography*. Mankato, MN: Bridgestone, 2002.

Osborne, Mary Pope. *American Tall Tales*. New York: Knopf, 1991.

Parks, Aileen Wells. *Davy Crockett*. New York: Aladdin, 1986.

Schanzer, Rosalyn. *Davy Crockett Saves the World*. New York: HarperCollins, 2001.

Stoutenburg, Adrien. *American Tall Tales*. New York: Puffin, 1976.

Exploring Encyclopedias

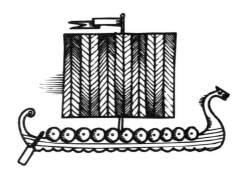

To explore an encyclopedia, use the index and guidewords to make the exploring go more quickly. Guidewords guide you to a certain page from the top of pages. The index is located in one volume to guide you to a certain page.

Use the encyclopedia to see what the following explorers discovered.

Search without the index (Just try to select the right volumes.)

Explorer	Volume Number:	What the explorer found:
1. Hernando Cortes	_____	_____
2. Hernando de Soto	_____	_____
3. Jacques Cartier	_____	_____
4. Francisco Pizarro	_____	_____

Search *with the index* (Use the index to find the correct volumes and pages, and then look up the answer.)

Explorer	Encyclopedia Page:	What the explorer found:
5. Amerigo Vespuccui	_____	_____
6. Henry Hudson	_____	_____

Exploring Encyclopedias

Standards

Students will

- Use encyclopedias to gather information. (McREL 2)
- Use electronic media to gather information (e.g. Internet, videos). (McREL 4)
- Use keywords, guidewords, alphabetical and numerical order, indexes, cross references, and letters on volumes to find information for research topics. (McREL 5)
- Access information efficiently and effectively. (AASL/AECT 1)
- Evaluate information critically and competently. (AASL/AECT 2)
- Use information effectively and creatively. (AASL/AECT 3)
- Pursue information related to personal interests. (AASL/AECT 4)
- Recognize the importance of information to a democratic society. (AASL/AECT 7)

Objectives

Students review encyclopedia use and search for various explorers' discoveries.

Directions

1. The library teacher reviews how to use an encyclopedia, including the use of guide-words and index. The teacher reminds students that they need to look under the last name of a person when using an encyclopedia.
2. The social studies teacher shows students how to find the correct volume, and read a couple facts about an explorer.
3. Teachers emphasize that the top part of the worksheet is answered without using the index, and bottom part is answered using the encyclopedia index.
4. When completed, students may go online to research and add more information.

Learning Styles

Linguistic (reading and writing), mathematical (thinking logically), interpersonal (working in groups)

Teaching Team

Library, and social studies teachers

Suggested Sources

World Book. *World Book Encyclopedia*. Chicago, ILL: World Book, 2005.
http://www.encyclopedia.com
http://www.kidskonnect.com/Encyclopedia

Surfing, Surfing

Do you know these Internet surfing skills (to find Internet things)?

1. First, type a word (or several words) in the Search or Find box.
2. Second, combine search words using a Boolean connector (such as *and, or, not*).
3. No luck? Try a different search engine.

Try some Internet surfing!

1. List some search engines: _____

   _____

2. Type the address of a search engine and push enter. Then type the word *Lincoln* in the Search (or Find) box search. How many choices or sites were found for Abraham Lincoln? _____

3. Combine the word *Lincoln* with another word with a Boolean connector. For example, try typing *Lincoln* and *the Civil War* How many choices were there? _____

4. Type a different search engine and then repeat the same searches. How many different choices or sites were found this time? _____

5. How did the surfing go? Which surfing skills gave the most results?

   _____

   _____

Surfing, Surfing

Standards

Students will

- Write in a variety of forms of genre. (McREL 1)
- Use electronic media to gather information (e.g. Internet, videos). (McREL 4)
- Access information efficiently and effectively. (AASL/AECT 1)
- Evaluate information critically and competently. (AASL/AECT 2)
- Recognize the importance of information to a democratic society. (AASL/AECT 7)
- Practice ethical behavior in regard to information and information technology. (AASL/AECT 8)

Objectives

Students discuss and use Internet searching skills.

Directions

1. The computer or library teacher lead a student discussion on how to search the Internet using the skills listed on the student worksheet. Encourage students to narrow or enlarge wording for word searches if needed. Searching suggestions may also be found online at many sites including KidsClick at http://www.rcls.org/wows.
2. Students search the Internet using the searching skills to answer worksheet questions.
3. Students share answers.
4. If time permits, students may locate and/or share other searching tips.
5. Teachers may want to discuss Internet safety for kids at http://www.netsmartz.org.

Learning Styles

Linguistic (reading, writing), mathematical (computers), and intrapersonal (working alone)

Teaching Teams

Computer and library teachers

Suggested Sources

Internet Safety and Search Tip Sites:
http://www.netsmartz.org
http://www.rcls.org/wows

Catching Indian/Native American Folktales

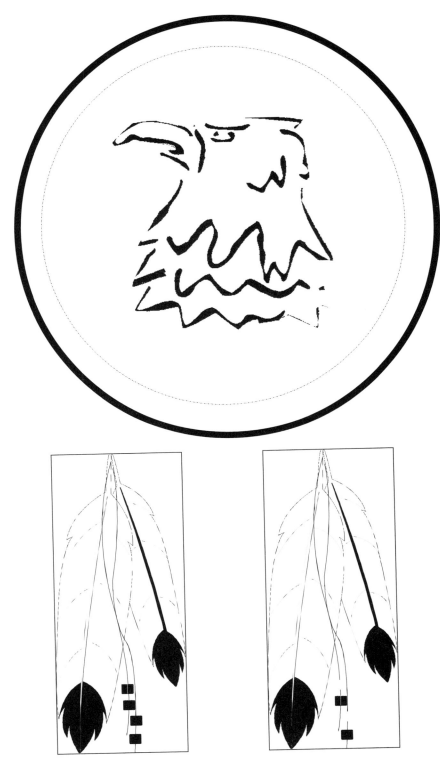

Catching Indian/Native American Folktales

Standards

Students will

- Use reading skills and strategies to understand a variety of familiar literary passages and text (e.g. fairy tales, folktales, fiction, nonfiction, fables, legends, poems, biographies). (McCREL 7).
- Know the elements that compose a story. (e.g. character, plot, events, setting). (McREL 8)
- Appreciate and enjoy literature and other creative expressions of information. (AASL/AECT 5)
- Recognize the importance of information to a democratic society. (AASL/AECT 7)
- Participate effectively in groups to pursue and generate information. (AASL/AECT 9)

Objectives

Students discuss main plot, setting, and main characters of an Indian/Native American folktale. Students create a wind catcher.

Directions

1. Copy student worksheets onto stiff or card stock paper.
2. The library teacher reads or tells an Indian/ Native American folktale.
3. After hearing the story, the class discusses plot, setting, and main characters.
4. The teacher explains that eagles have a special meaning for some traditional North American Indian tribes, tied to spirituality, peace, and/or unity.
5. The art teacher shows students how to make an Indian/North American traditional eagle wind catcher. Color the worksheet eagle and feathers, and then cut out a narrow half-inch circular pattern inside the eagle circle rim, leaving a short portion attached at the top. Attach a transparent color film or tissue paper on the back of the circle. Attach the feather strips to the bottom of the circle with thin metal wires or ribbons. Finally attach a thin wire or ribbon to the top of the wind catcher as a hanger.

Learning Styles

Spatial (creating art work), interpersonal (discussing together), and intrapersonal (working alone)

Teaching Team

Art and library teachers

Suggested Sources

Bruchac, Joseph. *The First Strawberries*. New York: Dial, 1993.
Bruchac, Joseph and Gayle Ross. *The Story of the Milky Way*. New York: Dial, 1995.
Goble, Paul *Her Seven Brothers*. New York: Bradbury Press, 1988.

Midnight Ride

A narrative poem tells a story. Read the narrative poem of *The Midnight Ride of Paul Revere*. Then summarize the plot by creating your own rhyming narrative poem.

_____

_____

_____

_____

_____

_____

_____

Midnight Ride

Standards

Students will

- Use reading skills and strategies to understand a variety of familiar literary passages and text (e.g. fairy tales, folktales, fiction, nonfiction, fables, legends, poems, biographies). (McCREL 7)
- Know the elements that compose a story. (e.g. character, plot, events, setting). (McREL 8)
- Appreciate and enjoy literature and other creative expressions of information. (AASL/AECT 5)
- Recognize the importance of information to a democratic society. (AASL/AECT 7)
- Participate effectively in groups to pursue and generate information. (AASL/AECT 9)

Objectives

Students discuss the plot and events of *The Midnight Ride of Paul Revere*. Students write a narrative poem of the main plot.

Directions

1. The library or language arts teacher reads *The Midnight Ride of Paul Revere*, and explains that the story is a narrative poem.
2. Students discuss the main plot and major events for a poem.
3. Small groups of students write a four-line narrative rhyming poem summarizing the main plot of the story.
4. After students have shared poems, the poems maybe displayed.

Learning Styles

Linguistic (writing), intrapersonal (working alone), and interpersonal (working together)

Teaching Team

Language arts and library teachers

Suggested Sources

Longfellow, Henry Wadsworth and Christopher Bing. *The Midnight Ride of Paul Revere*. New York: Handprint Books, 2001.
Longfellow, Henry Wadsworth and Ted Rand. *Paul Reveres' Ride*. New York: Dutton, 1990.

The Challenge

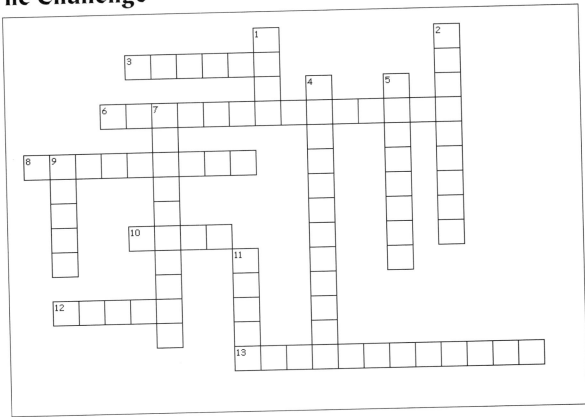

Take the Challenge! Answer these questions in the puzzle:

Across

3. Nonfiction books are shelved _____
6. Fiction books are shelved by _____
8. A book about a person
10. Biography books are shelved by the _____ name of the subject/person
12. A reference book used for maps
13. A reference book containing information about a person/place/thing

Down

1. Nonfiction books: True or False?
2. The date of a book is:
4. A list of sources to credit the authors
5. A book part that defines words
7. Copying work without giving proper credit is called _____
9. Book part in the back that give subjects and page numbers.
11. Fiction books: True or False?

From Joyce Keeling, *Lesson Plans for the Busy Librarian: A Standards Based Approach for the Elementary Library Media Center*, Volume 2. Westport, CT: Libraries Unlimited. © 2006.

The Challenge

Standards

Students will

- Write in a variety of forms of genre. (McREL 1)
- Use various parts of a book. (McREL 9)
- Strive for excellence in information seeking and knowledge generation. (AASL/AECT 6)
- Recognize the importance of information to a democratic society. (AASL/AECT 7)
- Practice ethical behavior in regard to information and information technology. (AASL/AECT 8)
- Participate in groups to pursue and generate information. (AASL/AECT 9)

Objectives

Students review aspects of the library. Students complete a crossword puzzle.

Directions

1. The language arts and library teachers review the following facts: Nonfiction books are *true*; The date of a book is *copyright*; Nonfiction books are shelved by *number*; List of sources that a person used, which will credit the authors is the *bibliography*; A book part that defines words is the *glossary*; Fiction books are shelved *alphabetically*; Copying work illegally is called *plagiarism*; A book about a person is a *biography*; A book part with page numbers and subjects in back is the *index*; Biography books are shelved by *last* name of the subject or person that it is about; Fiction books are *false*; A reference book used for maps is an *atlas*; A reference book that has information about a person, place or thing is the *encyclopedia*.

2. List crossword puzzle words on the board: true, false, copyright, number, alphabetically, bibliography, glossary, plagiarism, biography, index, last, atlas, encyclopedia.

3. Students may work with a partner to complete the crossword puzzle.

4. Teachers check students' work for excellence in learning.

Learning Styles

Mathematical (challenging work), linguistic (writing), and interpersonal (working with others)

Teaching Team

Language arts and library teachers

Suggested Sources

None needed

Journaling with Lewis and Clark

Search Lewis and Clark's journey. How did Lewis and Clark find their way across the United States in 1804 without a map? Write 5 facts in a journal entry like they did (write facts with dates).

The Journal of Lewis and Clark

From Joyce Keeling, *Lesson Plans for the Busy Librarian: A Standards Based Approach for the Elementary Library Media Center*, Volume 2. Westport, CT: Libraries Unlimited. © 2006.

Journaling with Lewis and Clark

Standards

Students will

- Write in a variety of forms of genre. (McREL 1)
- Use reading skills and strategies to understand a variety of familiar literary passages and text (e.g. fairy tales, folktales, fiction, nonfiction, fables, legends, poems, biographies). (McREL 7)
- Access information efficiently and effectively. (AASL/AECT 1)
- Evaluate information critically and competently. (AASL/AECT 2)
- Use information effectively and creatively. (AASL/AECT 3)
- Practice ethical behavior in regard to information and information technology. (AASL/AECT 8)

Objectives

Students research Lewis and Clark's journey and write journal entries.

Directions

1. The social studies teacher reviews the story of Lewis and Clark and explains that the explorers wrote of their experiences in a journal.
2. The library teacher introduces resources the students will use.
3. Small groups research Lewis and Clark, and then write five facts and dates on their worksheet journals.
4. In Art, students glue their journal sheets on brown paper sack sheets and crinkled slightly to look old. Use string or twine to tie around journals.

Learning Styles

Linguistic (reading, writing), mathematical (thinking logically), spatial (imaging), interpersonal (working with others), and intrapersonal (working alone)

Teaching Team

Art, library, and social studies teachers

Suggested Sources

Bowen, Andy R. *The Story of Beyond. A Story of Lewis and Clark*. Minneapolis, MN: Lerner, 1997.

Grags, Rod. *Lewis and Clark On the Trail of Discovery*. Nashville, Tenn: Rutledge Hill Press, 2003.

Schanzer, Rosalyn. *How We Crossed the West. The Adventure of Lewis and Clark*. Washington D.C.: National Geographic Society, 2002.

Sullivan, George. *In Their Own Words Lewis and Clark*. New York: Scholastic, 2000.

Winters, Patti. *The Expedition of Lewis and Clark Videorecording as told by Meriwether Lewis*. El Dorado, CA: 100% Educational Videos, 2001.

http://www.lewis-clark.org

Calling in a Good Christmas Tree

Decorate the tree with titles from every Dewey Decimal category.

Put the category number on the white ball and put the book title on the line.

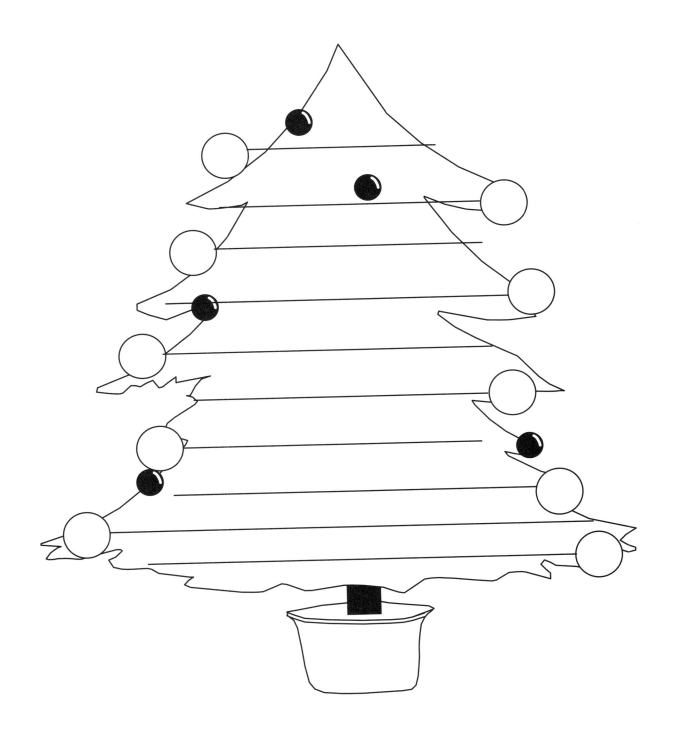

Calling in a Good Christmas Tree

Standards

Students will

- Write in a variety of forms of genre. (McREL 1)
- Use reading skills and strategies to understand a variety of familiar literary passages and text (e.g. fairy tales, folktales, fiction, nonfiction, fables, legends, poems, biographies). (McREL 7)
- Pursue information related to personal interests. (AASL/AECT 4)
- Strive for excellence in information seeking and knowledge generation. (AASL/AECT 6)
- Recognize the importance of information to a democratic society. (AASL/AECT 7)
- Participate in groups to pursue and generate information. (AASL/AECT 9)

Objectives

Students write the titles of nonfiction books from every Dewey Decimal category.

Directions

1. Copy student worksheets on green paper.
2. The library teacher instructs students to find and write down books they would personally recommend from every major Dewey Decimal category. The nonfiction books may be ones already read and enjoyed, or students may browse and pick titles from the shelves. Students may want to include some Christmas books on cooking, crafts, customs, poems, etc.
3. Student pairs decorate their worksheet trees by writing the book call numbers on the balls and the book titles on the (garland) lines.
4. Teachers monitor and check students for excellence in work performance. Display the worksheets in the school library.

Learning Styles

Linguistic (writing, reading) and interpersonal (working with others)

Teaching Team

Language arts and library teachers

Suggested Sources

Crocker, Betty. *Betty Crocker's Best Christmas Cookbook.* New York: Macmillan 1999. [600s]
Livingston, Myra Cohn. *Christmas Poems.* New York: Holiday House, 1984. [800s]
McKissack, Pat. *Christmas in the Big House.* NY: Scholastic, 1994. [900s]
Ray, Jane. *The Story of Christmas.* New York: Dutton, 1991. [200s]
Robinson, Fay. *Christmas Crafts.* Berkeley Heights, NJ: Enslow, 2004. [700s]

Time Travel

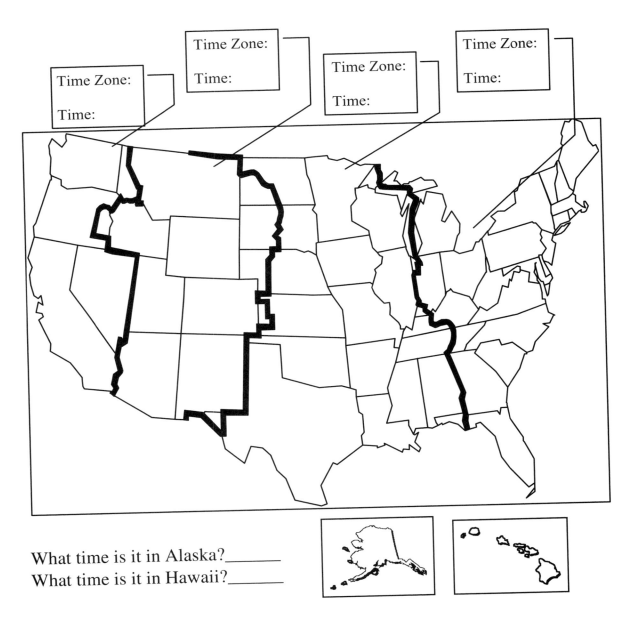

Traveling takes time! Use an atlas! Find the differences of time across the United States. Write the time zone and the clock time for each area. Don't forget the time in Alaska and Hawaii. Once you have taken time to do that, see how long it takes you to label the states on the map.

Time Zone:

Time:

Time Zone:

Time:

Time Zone:

Time:

Time Zone:

Time:

What time is it in Alaska?_____
What time is it in Hawaii?_____

How many states did you label? _____   Good Job!

From Joyce Keeling, *Lesson Plans for the Busy Librarian: A Standards Based Approach for the Elementary Library Media Center*, Volume 2. Westport, CT: Libraries Unlimited. © 2006.

Time Travel

Standards

Students will

- Write in a variety of forms of genre. (McREL 1)
- Use electronic media to gather information (e.g. Internet, videos). (McREL 4)
- Use a variety of resource materials to gather information for research topics (e.g. magazines, newspapers, dictionaries, schedules, journals, phone directories, globes, atlases, and almanacs). (McREL 6)
- Access information efficiently and effectively. (AASL/AECT 1)
- Evaluate information critically and competently. (AASL/AECT 2)
- Use information effectively and creatively. (AASL/AECT 3)
- Strive for excellence in information seeking and knowledge generation. (AASL/AECT 6)
- Recognize the importance of information to a democratic society. (AASL/AECT 7)
- Participate effectively in groups to pursue and generate information. (AASL/AECT 9)

Objectives

Students use atlases and maps, print or Internet versions, to locate U.S. time zones. They use the same sources to identify each state and label the map.

Directions

1. The social studies and library teachers explain time zones of the United States.
2. Student pairs locate the time zones and clock times on their maps.
3. Use a world atlas or Internet site such as *http://www.time.gov*.
4. After completing the times zones, student pairs label the states. Time students to see how many states are correctly labeled in the allotted time. Students may share their answers.

Learning Styles

Linguistic (reading, writing), mathematical (thinking logically, using computers), spatial (reading maps), and interpersonal (working in groups)

Teaching Team

Library and social studies teachers

Suggested Sources

Zeleny, Robert O, Ed. *World Book Atlas.* Chicago, Ill: World Book, 2004.
Time Zone Site:
http://www.time.gov

Help Rapunzel

senaehgiantthandsomezigpatrarausiyymmtrintuib
ittshoemakgrrlimagddrgshanselandgretaltuypyeio
ntugyugcipoicprisonrabtrsepiglkoplceoppolizeeiy
gkcajteeeakonbabynigtuyprincegweouhsmrdpoiir
iaehdragondkrwiwentredrreeibftsoreamjhynntiiit
nsihtaporgbkinefllindrtrapunzelmusbamobkciiico
gocouplerlrmacerfairygodmotheriprnilekliogeiiiw
gunlbeautifulloxttnnsnowwhitertttcatiiiaskmnttie
clbtsejlongthairrveidesabcinderelawitchyivrjibpir

1. Help Rapunzel out of the tower! Help by searching for the words from her story. Find and circle these words in the box above (They are hidden across and up and down):

| Rapunzel | tower | singing | prince | handsome | witch |
| beautiful | long | hair | baby | couple | |

2. Now rewrite a short story of Rapunzel using the words you found, while adding some of your own words.

Help Rapunzel

Standards

Students will

- Write in a variety of genres. (McREL 1)
- Use reading skills and strategies to understand a variety of familiar literary passages and text (e.g., fairy tales, folktales, fiction, nonfiction, fables, legends, poems, biographies). (McREL 7)
- Know the elements that compose a story (e.g., character, plot, events, setting). (McREL 8)
- Appreciate and enjoy literature and other creative expressions of information. (AASL/AECT 5)

Objectives

Students discuss *Rapunzel*. They complete a word search puzzle. Students write their own short story version of the tale using the words from the puzzle.

Directions

1. The library or reading teacher reads the *Rapunzel* fairy tale, followed by a discussion of main plot, characters, and events.
2. Students complete a word search about *Rapunzel*.
3. Using the words from the puzzle, and adding words of their own, students write a short version of the story.
4. Stories are shared with the class.

Learning Styles

Linguistic (reading, writing), mathematical (thinking logically), and intrapersonal (working alone).

Teaching Team

Library and reading teachers.

Suggested Sources

Martin, Annie-Claude (ill.). *A Treasury of Fairy Tales*. Oxfordshire, England: Transedition, 1995.

Rowe, Gavin (ill.). *Fairy Tales*. Newmarket, England: Brimax, 1996.

Zelinsky, Paul O. *Rapunzel*. New York: Dutton, 1997.

Famous Facts

The *Famous First Facts* book and the almanac have facts that are well known throughout the country and world. The *Famous First Facts* covers facts about America, and the almanac has millions of facts about the whole world. Use both references to find the following facts.

Use *Famous First Facts*

1. When was glass invented? _____

2. When was the football made? _____

3. When was the escalator created? _____
   Who made it? _____

4. When was the steam engine invented? _____
   Who made it? _____

5. When were lasers created? _____
   Who created them? _____

Just ask yourself! If you became famous for an invention, what would it be?

_____

Use *The World Almanac and Book of Facts*

1. Who invented radar? _____ What year? _____

2. Who discovered the X-ray? _____ What year? _____

3. Find any other interesting fact in the almanac.

Famous Facts

Standards

Students will

- Write in a variety of genres. (McREL 1)
- Use a variety of resource materials to gather information for research topics (e.g., magazines, newspapers, dictionaries, schedules, journals, phone directories, globes, atlases, and almanacs). (McREL 6)
- Access information efficiently and effectively. (AASL/AECT 1)
- Evaluate information critically and competently. (AASL/AECT 2)
- Use information effectively and creatively. (AASL/AECT 3)
- Pursue information related to personal interests. (AASL/AECT 4)
- Strive for excellence in information seeking and knowledge generation. (AASL/AECT 6)
- Recognize the importance of information to a democratic society. (AASL/AECT 7)
- Participate effectively in groups to pursue and generate information. (AASL/AECT 9)

Objectives

Students use *Famous First Facts* and almanacs to find inventors and inventions.

Directions

1. The library teacher introduces *Famous First Facts* and almanacs, and explains how to use them.
2. The social studies teacher reviews some inventors and inventions.
3. Teachers assist small groups in using *Famous First Facts* and almanacs to answer questions about inventions and inventors.
4. Students may share their answers.

Learning Styles

Linguistic (reading, writing, trivia) and interpersonal (working in groups).

Teaching Team

Library and social studies teachers.

Suggested Sources

Kane, Joseph Nathan. *Famous First Facts* [*Famous First Facts: A Record of First Happenings, Discoveries and Inventions in American History*]. New York: H.W. Wilson, 1997.

McGeveran, William Jr. (dir.). *The World Almanac and Book of Facts 2004*. New York: World Almanac, 2004.

Chinese Folklore

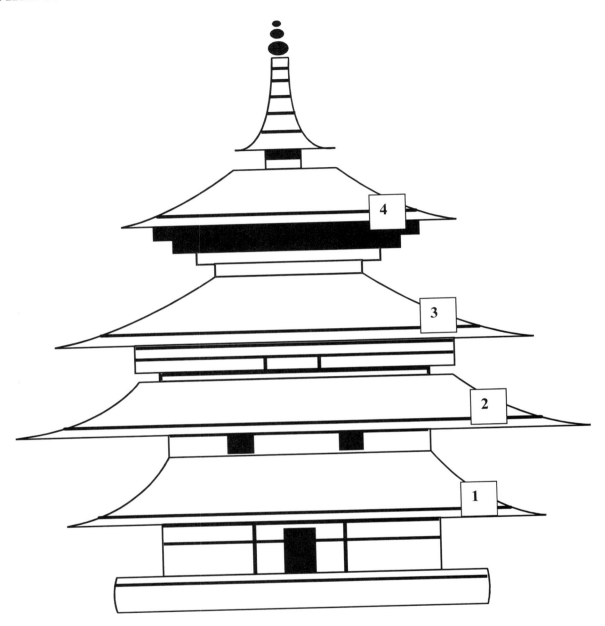

Listen to a Chinese folktale. Write your answers on the building:

1. Write the title on the first level of the building.

2. Summarize, in one sentence, the main plot on the second level.

3. List the main characters on the third level.

4. Briefly describe the theme on the fourth level.

From Joyce Keeling, *Lesson Plans for the Busy Librarian: A Standards Based Approach for the Elementary Library Media Center*, Volume 2. Westport, CT: Libraries Unlimited. © 2006.

Chinese Folklore

Standards

Students will

- Write in a variety of genres. (McREL 1)
- Use reading skills and strategies to understand a variety of familiar literary passages and text (e.g., fairy tales, folktales, fiction, nonfiction, fables, legends, poems, biographies). (McREL 7)
- Know the elements that compose a story (e.g., character, plot, events, setting). (McREL 8)
- Appreciate and enjoy literature and other creative expressions of information. (AASL/AECT 5)

Objectives

Students listen to a Chinese folktale and discuss it. They answer questions on plot, character, theme, and title.

Directions

1. The library or reading teacher reads the folktale.
2. Teachers discuss theme(s) and other literary elements of the folktale.
3. Students answer questions on theme, title, characters, and main plot, writing their answers on each level of the oriental building.
4. When worksheets are completed, the class discusses their answers.

Learning Styles

Linguistic (writing), interpersonal (discussing), and intrapersonal (working alone).

Teaching Team

Library and reading teachers.

Suggested Sources

Perlman, Janet. *Seven Chinese Brothers*. New York: Scholastic, 1990.
Yep, Laurence. *The Man Who Tricked a Ghost*. Mahwah, NJ: Bridgewater, 1993.
Yep, Laurence. *Tiger Woman*. Mahwah, NJ: Bridgewater, 1995.

Presidents

Researching a President

Your president: _____ Your name:_____

I. Use a biography book to answer these questions:

(1) When was your president born? _____

(2) Where was he born? _____

(3) What was his career before being president? _____

(4) Bibliographic information on your book:

Author:_____

Title:_____   Publishing Place: _____

Publisher: _____   Copyright:_____

II. Use an encyclopedia database to answer these:

(1) When was he president of the United States? _____

(2) Name two things he did as president:

A. _____

B. _____

(3) Bibliographic information on the Database:

Subject: _____   Database: _____

Date:_____

III. Type your presidential information. Type two paragraphs.

(1) Type the name of your president for the title.

(2) Type the information from the book in the first paragraph.

Type the information from the database in the second paragraph.

IV. Use the Internet http://www.whitehouse.gov site for a picture.

(1) Add a picture to your research paper.

(2) Bibliographic information on your Internet site:

Author:_____   Subject: _____

Date:_____   Web Site: _____

Presidents

Standards

Students will

- Write in a variety of genres. (McREL 1)
- Use encyclopedias to gather information. (McREL 2)
- Use electronic media to gather information (e.g., Internet, videos). (McREL 4)
- Access information efficiently and effectively. (AASL/AECT 1)
- Evaluate information critically and competently. (AASL/AECT 2)
- Use information effectively and creatively. (AASL/AECT 3)
- Recognize the importance of information to a democratic society. (AASL/AECT 7)
- Practice ethical behavior in regard to information and information technology. (AASL/AECT 8)

Objectives

Students research a president using a book, the Internet, and an online encyclopedia database. Using computers, they type two paragraphs and attach a picture.

Directions

1. This lesson will take two class periods.
2. The social studies teacher assigns president topics to student pairs.
3. Student pairs answer their questions using a book, encyclopedia database, and the Internet, with the assistance of teachers. Students are reminded of plagiarism.
4. After completing the worksheets, students type the section one answers in their first paragraph, and then type the section two answers in their second paragraph.
5. Students insert a picture from an Internet site onto their page and add a title.

Learning Styles

Linguistic (reading and writing), mathematical (thinking logically), intrapersonal (typing), and interpersonal (researching in pairs).

Teaching Team

Library and social studies teachers.

Suggested Sources

Encyclopedia of Presidents [series]. Danbury, CT: Children's Press, 2003– .
Presidents MyReportLinks.com [series]. Berkeley Heights, NJ: Enslow Publishers, 2002– .
Presidential Leaders [set]. Minneapolis, MN: Lerner, 2003– .
U.S. Government White House Internet site: http://www.whitehouse.gov
Online database located at http://www.worldbookonline.com

Shark Attack Bibliography

When you use information from books, the Internet, or anywhere else, you must give credit for your sources. Always remember to locate the exact bibliographic information. Also watch spacing and punctuation! Here is an example of a bibliography from a student who researched sharks:

Bibliography

Anderson, Deb. "Shark Attacks." *Time*. 21 March 2005: 67–72.

Gould, Jan. *Great White Sharks*. Chicago: Albert White, 2004.

"Sharks." In *Encyclopedia Americana*. Vol. 10. New York: Oxford Press, 2004.

"Sharks." In *World Book Multimedia Encyclopedia*. Chicago: IL, 2005. [CD-ROM]

Solburg, Carisa. "Sharks Along the Pacific Rim." Available at *http://www.si.edu* [downloaded 21 May 2004].

- -

Look at the shark bibliography to answer these questions:

1. What are the sources in italics? _____

2. What things have quotations marks around them? _____

3. How many spaces are there after periods? _____
   How many spaces are there before the second entry line?____

4. Next to each bibliography entry, label the source. Write Internet, CD-ROM, magazine, book, or encyclopedia.

Shark Attack Bibliography

Standards

Students will

- Write in a variety of genres. (McREL 1)
- Evaluate information critically and competently. (AASL/AECT 2)
- Recognize the importance of information to a democratic society. (AASL/AECT 7)
- Practice ethical behavior in regard to information and information technology. (AASL/AECT 8)
- Participate effectively in groups to pursue and generate information. (AASL/AECT 9)

Objectives

Students answer questions about a bibliography, then type a bibliography on computers.

Directions

1. Copy the worksheet onto an overhead transparency so it can be used for instruction.
2. The library teacher explains that a bibliography lists sources used for a report, and that correct punctuation and information is very important. Using the overhead worksheet, the language arts teacher explains the information required in bibliography entries, and the correct formatting of the information.
3. On their worksheets, student pairs answer questions regarding the (fictitious) worksheet bibliography. Teachers check students' work for understanding.
4. After completing their worksheets, students type a bibliography, using their worksheet as a guide. They may either type a bibliography from the sources used in their presidential report, or use sources for another topic.

Learning Styles

Linguistic (reading and writing), mathematical (thinking logically), intrapersonal (working alone), and interpersonal (working in pairs).

Teaching Team

Language arts, library, and perhaps the social studies teaching team.

Suggested Sources

Word processing program.
Completed presidential report worksheets.

Sea Monster

Read the following Greek legend. After reading it, lightly cross off 5–8 adjectives in the story. Use a thesaurus to find a synonym or antonym for each adjective. Write the synonym or antonym above your crossed-off word. Then read your new story. Did you make it more exciting or funny?

Long, long ago there was a beautiful queen named Cassiopeia. Her daughter Andromeda was pretty too. The queen boasted that she and her daughter were prettier than the sea nymphs in the deep blue sea!

Many pretty sea nymphs heard the queen. So they sent a frightening sea monster. The queen's people were scared! They couldn't fish anymore, because the horrible, green sea creature would sink their boats.

The worried king asked the sea nymphs how to get rid of the sea monster. They said that the lovely Andromeda would have to be eaten by the terrifying monster. So, Andromeda sadly went out to the sea monster.

Luckily a handsome young man called Perseus was flying by and saw Andromeda. With great strength and courage, he saved her. So the sea nymphs turned the king, queen, princess, and Perseus into stars in the sky!

From Joyce Keeling, *Lesson Plans for the Busy Librarian: A Standards Based Approach for the Elementary Library Media Center*, Volume 2. Westport, CT: Libraries Unlimited. © 2006.

Sea Monster

Standards

Students will

- Write in a variety of genres. (McREL 1)
- Use reading skills and strategies to understand a variety of familiar literary passages and text (e.g., fairy tales, folktales, fiction, nonfiction, fables, legends, poems, biographies). (McREL 7)
- Access information efficiently and effectively. (AASL/AECT 1)
- Use information effectively and creatively. (AASL/AECT 3)
- Appreciate and enjoy literature and other creative expression of information. (AASL/AECT 5)
- Strive for excellence in information seeking and knowledge generation. (AASL/AECT 6)

Objectives

Students read and discuss a Greek legend. Students use a thesaurus to replace adjectives within the story.

Directions

1. The library teacher reviews how to use a thesaurus.
2. Students read the Greek legend from their student worksheets. The class discusses events, plot, and characters.
3. The reading teacher defines the term *adjective*. Students lightly cross out five to eight adjectives in the story. They replace those adjectives with a synonym or antonym found in a thesaurus. They may find adjectives that give the story a humorous slant. Students may work in small groups if copies of sources are limited. Teachers will assist.
4. Students enjoy retelling the story to the class.

Learning Styles

Mathematical (thinking logically), linguistic (writing), spatial (creating, imagining), interpersonal (working with others), and intrapersonal (working alone).

Teaching Team

Library and reading teachers.

Suggested Sources

Morris, Christopher (ed.). *The Harcourt Brace Student Thesaurus*. New York: Harcourt Brace, 1994.

Roget's International Thesaurus. 5th ed. New York: HarperCollins, 1992.

Roget's Student Thesaurus. Glenview, IL: Scott Foresman, 2000.

Shakespeare's *Romeo and Juliet* ~ Reader's Theatre

Readers: Romeo, Juliet's Father, Priest, Old Nurse, Juliet, and the Narrator. The readers must read with emotion!

Narrator: This is the story of two teens from the Montague and Capulet families. Their families always fought with each other. There was the handsome seventeen-year-old Montague son named Romeo. Then there was the pretty red-haired fourteen-year-old Capulet girl named Juliet.

Scene I: The Party

Narrator: Romeo and his friends hear about a party and go in disguise. When the music begins, pretty Juliet comes down the stairs in a sparkling green gown. Even though they did not know each other, Romeo and Juliet fall in love right away. Eventually Juliet asks her old nurse to find out who Romeo is.

Romeo: What do you need, Old Nurse?

Old Nurse: Juliet wants to know who you are!

Romeo: You must tell no one, but my lovely Juliet. I am Romeo, from the Montague family!

Narrator: The nurse told Juliet. Juliet was scared since Romeo's family were the enemies of her family.

Scene II: Love

Narrator: One night Juliet lay awake in her room thinking of Romeo, when there was a noise outside her bedroom window.

Juliet: My Romeo is here! I will go out to my bedroom balcony to see him.

Romeo: Oh, my Juliet, I love you. I want to marry you tomorrow!

Juliet: I love you, Romeo. I will marry you.

Scene III: The Wedding

Narrator: Romeo and Juliet go to the priest.

Priest: You wish me to marry you two? Are you sure? Juliet is so young!

Romeo: I love my Juliet and she loves me!

Juliet: I love you. I love you, my dear Romeo!

Priest: All right, I will marry you right now.

Narrator: After the wedding, Juliet goes to her home and Romeo goes to his

Scene IV: The Fight

Narrator: On his way to visit his secret bride, Juliet, Romeo gets into a fight. Something terrible happens. Now, he must tell his lovely Juliet goodbye.

Romeo: I was told that I must leave and never return. Your cousin attacked me in the street. I am sorry, but he died. I must go!

Juliet: No! No, stay! At least stay now.

Romeo: I will, but I must leave in the morning. I can never come back.

Scene V: The Deadly Plan

Narrator: Juliet goes to see the priest.

Juliet: Priest, Romeo is gone. Now, I am being forced to marry another.

Priest: Take this potion to make it look like you have died.

Narrator: Juliet takes the potion. Romeo never gets the message that explains that Juliet is still alive, and he only hears she is dead! Romeo rushes to his Juliet.

Romeo: [kneeling by Juliet] I'm back! Oh! My Juliet! She is dead! I can't stand it. I must take the poison.

Juliet: [wakes up] Oh, what a long sleep! Why is my handsome Romeo here? Oh, no! He's dead! I must use Romeo's dagger on myself!

Narrator: The families of Capulet and Montague are sad, but then learn to live in peace from the fatal tragedies of their Romeo and Juliet.

Discussion Questions

1. Who were the characters in the story?

2. Why was Juliet scared of loving Romeo? Why did they secretly marry?

3. How did the priest help Juliet?

4. What kind of lesson did you learn from the story?

5. Change the story! Draw or write a happy ending here:

Shakespeare's *Romeo and Juliet* ~ Reader's Theatre

Standards

Students will

- Use reading skills and strategies to understand a variety of familiar literary passages and text (e.g., fairy tales, folktales, fiction, nonfiction, fables, legends, poems, biographies). (McREL 7)
- Appreciate and enjoy literature and other creative expression of information. (AASL/AECT 5)
- Participate effectively in groups to pursue and generate information. (AASL/AECT 9)

Objectives

Student groups act out a *Romeo and Juliet* reader's theatre.

Directions

1. This lesson will take two class periods.
2. The library and reading teachers explain that students will act out a reader's theatre production of *Romeo and Juliet.*
3. The class reads and discusses the play, and then answers the worksheet questions.
4. Groups of six to eight students act out the reader's theatre. Roles are assigned, including that of a leader or producer.
5. Student groups practice reading the story with emotion, volume, and clarity.
6. Student groups perform the reader's theatre during the next class.

Learning Styles

Linguistic (writing, reading), spatial (creating, imagining), interpersonal (working in groups), and intrapersonal (working alone).

Teaching Team

Library and reading teachers.

Suggested Sources

None needed.

Read All About It!

Read all about it in newspapers!

A good newspaper story has a catchy headline. It also answers the questions **who, what, when, where,** and **why**.

Read a newspaper article. Then let's hear about it! Tell about your article:

1. **What** was the headline _____

2. **Who** was in the story? _____

3. **When** did the story take place? _____

4. **Where** did it happen?_____

5. **What** happened in the story? _____

   _____

   _____

6. **Why** did things in the story happen? _____

   _____

   _____

7. Write a newspaper bibliography description for your article. Make it like the following example:

"Surfing the Waves." *Des Moines News.* 15 June 2006, sec. 3, p. 23.

   _____

   _____

From Joyce Keeling, *Lesson Plans for the Busy Librarian: A Standards Based Approach for the Elementary Library Media Center*, Volume 2. Westport, CT: Libraries Unlimited. © 2006.

Read All About It!

Standards

Students will

- Write in a variety of forms of genre. (McREL 1)
- Use electronic media to gather information (e.g. Internet, videos). (McREL 4)
- Use a variety of resources to gather information for research topics (e.g. magazines, newspapers, dictionaries, schedules, journals, phone directories, globes, atlases, and almanacs). (McREL 6)
- Access information efficiently and effectively. (AASL/AECT 1)
- Evaluate information critically and competently. (AASL/AECT 2)
- Use information effectively and creatively. (AASL/AECT 3)
- Recognize the importance of information to a democratic society. (AASL/AECT 7)
- Participate effectively in groups to pursue and generate information. (AASL/AECT 9)

Objectives

Students discuss and find the "who, what, where, why, and when" of a newspaper article. They write a newspaper bibliography.

Directions

1. The language arts and reading teachers explain that a newspaper story answers "who, what, where, when, and why." It also has a catchy headline. Teachers show examples of newspaper articles.
2. The library teacher describes how to write a newspaper bibliography as shown on the bottom of the student worksheets.
3. Small student groups find a newspaper article and use it to answer the worksheet questions.
4. Students attach their newspaper article to their worksheets.

Learning Styles

Linguistic (reading, writing), mathematical (using computers), interpersonal (working in groups), and intrapersonal (working alone)

Teaching Team

Language arts and library teachers

Suggested Sources

Online Newspapers:
http://www.dmregister.com
http://nytimes.com
http://www.onlinenewspapers.com [tells of many online newspapers]

Touring a Country

To tour a new country, you need to research it and then make a pocket tourist brochure!

For the inside of the brochure: (1) Find and write facts. (2) Cut on the outside solid line. (3) Fold on the center dotted line. (4) Add small Internet pictures.

Language: (Use an Almanc)	**2–3 Tourist Places:** (Use an Encyclopedia-Note Pictures)
Money (Monetary Unit): (Use an Almanc)	
A Geographic Place: **A Major City:** (Use an Atlas)	**Weather:** (Use an Encyclopedia)

For the outside of your brochure: Write down your country's name on the front in large letters. Add an Internet picture.

From Joyce Keeling, *Lesson Plans for the Busy Librarian: A Standards Based Approach for the Elementary Library Media Center*, Volume 2. Westport, CT: Libraries Unlimited. © 2006.

Touring a Country

Standards

Students will

- Write in a variety of genres. (McREL 1)
- Use encyclopedias to gather information. (McREL 2)
- Use electronic media to gather information (e.g., Internet, videos). (McREL 4)
- Use a variety of resources to gather information for research topics (e.g., magazines, newspapers, dictionaries, schedules, journals, phone directories, globes, atlases, and almanacs). (McREL 6)
- Access information efficiently and effectively. (AASL/AECT 1)
- Evaluate information critically and competently. (AASL/AECT 2)
- Use information effectively and creatively. (AASL/AECT 3)
- Recognize the importance of information to a democratic society. (AASL/AECT 7)

Objectives

Student pairs create a tourist brochure from their worksheets by researching the country using an encyclopedia, atlas, almanac, and the Internet.

Directions

1. This lesson may take two lessons.
2. The social studies teacher has student pairs chose a country and make travel brochures.
3. The library teacher explains that students will use an almanac to find their country capital and currency, and an atlas to find geographic places and cities. Finally, they will use an encyclopedia to find tourist places and find their country's weather.
4. They add small online country pictures to their brochures. The brochures are cut out and folded on the dotted lines. The country's name is put on the front with the student's name.
5. Students display their brochures in the library or main classroom.

Learning Styles

Linguistic (writing), spatial (reading maps), and interpersonal (group work).

Teaching Team

Library and social studies teachers.

Suggested Sources

McGeveran, William Jr. (dir.). *The World Almanac and Book of Facts 2004*. New York: World Almanac, 2004

Zeleny, Robert O. *World Book Atlas*. Chicago, IL: World Book, 2004.

World Book. *World Book Encyclopedia*. Chicago, IL: World Book, 2006.

A safe Internet site for many countries: http://yahooligans.yahoo.com/around_the_world/ countries/country_pictures

Bibliography

American Association of School Librarians and Association of Educational Communications and Technology. *Information Literacy Standards for Student Learning*. Chicago: American Library Association, 1998.

American Library Association and Association for Educational Communications and Technology. *Information Power: Building Partnerships for Learning*. Chicago: American Library Association, 1998.

American Library Association and Association for Educational Communications and Technology. *Information Power: Guidelines for School Library Media Programs*. Chicago: American Library Association, 1988.

Gardner, Howard. *Frames of Mind: Theory of Multiple Intelligences*. New York: Basic Books, 1983, 1993.

Kendall, John, Robert Moranzo, et al. *Content Knowledge*, 4th ed., 2004. Available online at http://www.mcrel.org/standards-benchmarks

Index

About the Author

JOYCE KEELING is a PreK-8 School Librarian at Clarion-Goldfield Schools where she has enjoyed teaching many library skills classes for over 10 years. She has a Masters degree in School Library from the University of Northern Iowa.